THE
PUREST
OF
PLEASURES

Designed by Roger Judd

Line illustrations by Wendy Brammall

Photographs by Andrew Lawson

British Library Cataloguing in Publication Data
Parker, Jill
 The purest of pleasures: the creation of
 a romantic garden.
 1. Gardening
 I. Title
 635   SB450.97

 ISBN 0-340-41605-X

Printed in Great Britain for Hodder & Stoughton Limited,
Mill Road, Dunton Green, Sevenoaks, Kent by
St Edmundsbury Press Limited, Bury St Edmunds, Suffolk.
Photoset by Rowland Phototypesetting Limited,
Bury St Edmunds, Suffolk.

Hodder & Stoughton Editorial Office: 47 Bedford Square,
London WC1B 3DP.

THE
PUREST
OF
PLEASURES

JILL PARKER

Hodder & Stoughton
LONDON SYDNEY AUCKLAND TORONTO

For Pat

Contents

Preface   7

1   *In Search of Romance*   10

2   *The Garden,*
or Grubbing About in the Herbaceous
Border   20

3   *The Orchard and its Terrace,*
or Taking Out a Hole   42

4   *Trees and Shrubs*   62

5   *The Coming of the Herb Garden*   72

6   *The Wild Garden,*
or Sowing Dragon's Teeth   84

7   *The Lake District*   90

8   *The Rose Connection*
(License my roving secateurs, and let
them go . . .)   120

9   *Family Feelings*   134

10   *Gardening:*
Doing it and Reading About it   154

11   *Time and the Place*   182

Index of Plants   191

Preface

For many years, I never knew I wanted a garden; in fact, I didn't own one at all. I always thought gardens simply existed. I used to visit my parents' home on a hillside in County Wicklow and to me the garden was merely 'out-of-doors', a beautiful extension of the place but nearly as static as the house itself.

I knew it was a focal thing for my parents – especially for my father – and to that I paid lipservice. I would Go Round, and even took on a bit of weeding or dead-heading to show willing, but I never dreamed that they were actually *making* their garden all the time.

My father was a very serious man but after a life of cosmopolitan affairs it probably amused him to see himself painstakingly hand-weeding for hours at a time in his old corduroys, stopping now and then for a contemplative smoke among his old roses. It was gardening for its own sake, a private contract between himself and his plants and one which was not achieving or ambitious in any sense – unless for the sake of the plants themselves. He grew his own vegetables, and it was a matter of honour not to spend money on the garden. He did have a feud with the grocer at Enniskerry about the quality of their respective sweet peas but that was the only competitiveness I ever detected. I have no idea where his love of gardening came from. It must have been a long-cherished desire which grew during his working life in cities, and was finally realised when he retired to his home ground in the Wicklow mountains.

With hindsight I begin to recognise in myself his style and to glimpse his attitude to gardening, and when I do I am reminded of Arthur Waley's translation of a poem, written in the early part of the ninth century, by the Governor of Chung-Chou, titled 'Planting Flowers on the Eastern Embankment'.

> I took money and bought flowering trees
> And planted them out on the bank to the east of the Keep.
> I simply bought whatever had most blooms,
> Not caring whether peach, apricot, or plum.
> A hundred fruits, all mixed up together:
> A thousand branches, flowering in due rotation.
> Each has its season coming early or late;
> But to each alike the fertile soil is kind.
> The red flowers hang like a heavy mist;
> The white flowers gleam like a fall of snow.
> The wandering bees cannot bear to leave them;
> The sweet birds also come there to roost.
> In front there flows an ever-running stream;
> Beneath there is a little flat terrace.
> Sometimes I sweep the flagstones of the terrace;
> Sometimes, in the wind, I raise my cup and drink.
> The flower-branches screen my head from the sun;
> The flower-buds fall down into my lap.
> Alone drinking, alone singing my songs,
> I do not notice that the moon is level with the steps.
> The people of Pa do not care for flowers;
> All the spring no one has come to look.
> But their Governor General, alone with his cup of wine
> Sits till evening and will not move from the place!

My father would not have spent the money, nor was he a Governor-General but apart from that, the poem might have been written about him.

Then my father died. Only weeks later we sat for the last time in the rickety bamboo chairs in the big old porch. It was ritual drinks-time and I poured whisky and water for the family solicitor who sat relaxed and friendly in my father's chair. The view was to the west – across the garden that melted into the meagre Irish fields and over Glencree to the hill on the far side. Outlined against the western sky and hunched into the shoulder of the hillside, the shapes of low gnarled trees were ancient animals. They were part of the family scene, the old animals, clambering and nudging along the skyline with their backs to the weather – always, unchangingly there.

After the helpful solicitor had driven away, I stood in the porch for the last time, and in the fading light I half expected the old creatures finally to shuffle off and make their lugubrious way round the side of the mountain, leaving as the rest of the family was leaving. Turning to look across the darkening garden, I suddenly realised how easily the old roses, standing in long grass, the borders with their tiers of flowers and the quiet lawns could dissolve and revert to nature, lost in the continuity of weeks of neglect. It was my first glimpse of the relationship between garden and gardener, and my first recognition of my own personal need for a garden, far more positive than a sad farewell in the Celtic twilight.

In the end, the garden I have spent the last thirteen years creating bears little resemblance to the Irish hillside garden in my mind's eye. I have abandoned that reality although not the spirit. The pursuit of it, however, has led me to the discovery of what Francis Bacon described as 'the purest of pleasures'.

In Search of Romance

ive years after that moment of recognition in my father's garden, I was still searching. We were full-time Londoners, and I was discovering that Irish hillside gardens are not to be found within range of a Friday afternoon's drive from London. I grew discouraged as the months went by and began to think that my garden did not exist. At last the penny dropped – I was right. My garden didn't exist. I had yet to make it. What I needed to find was the space. I recognised it instantly when I saw it – a very old and simple Cotswold farmhouse on the point of neglect.

We bought it at auction in October 1973.

'It'll need an awful lot doing to it,' was the doubtful reaction of friends. For me, that was the Main Attraction.

Bounded to the south by a medieval church and churchyard, with the ruined Minster rearing up at the back, the farm was part of a great thriving complex until the eighteenth century. Medieval barns and dovecot almost dwarf the house itself, and beyond them two meadows spread down to the little Windrush, running clean and fast to join the Thames above Oxford.

There was a faded, run-down air about it; it was not a self-confident place. There were spaces between the barns, behind the cowsheds, round the house, past the chicken runs and beyond the woodshed. The spaces and the buildings, standing in about five acres in all, had a continuity separate from the fields, though you couldn't call it a garden.

But walking through the small medieval house from the kitchen I reached a huge studded-oak door, and pulled it slowly open, needing the strength of both my arms. As it swung back a spread of long grass with two shallow stone steps at the end of a path and an old leaning apple-tree were held in the square stone door-frame, and I felt an inkling of magic. That could be a setting for a garden one day.

For a year we watched the garden-to-be with only sidelong glances, while the work and the excitement were directed at the house itself. It was a matter of scrapping partitions and uncovering fireplaces and ancient stone arches and putting in windows with deep sills. Living was a matter of campbeds, Primus stoves and thick plaster dust, and all the thrilling experiences of townees discovering fifteenth-century England, infinitely fascinating to themselves and infinitely boring to their friends.

In the Olden Days when the gentry built their country houses, their intention was to separate themselves from the land and the peasants who worked it. But a farm and its buildings were continuous with the land and the life of the farmer was the life of the land. So that living in a farmhouse made us aware not of a special, but of a most ordinary and almost total relationship with the countryside.

There were and still are stone walls everywhere, all
of the usual Cotswold four-foot and five-foot height.
Every view and every outlook extended into
meadows and over hedgerows, across may-trees and
lines of willows towards the river, with cattle standing
warm in summer buttercups or cold in autumn mists.
Near to the house where a wall leaned into the corner
of a barn, we began to see how the garden-to-be
would merge with the countryside.

The Cotswolds are full of stone anyway, and our
own particular corner had been built over for at least
seven centuries. Courtyards, stables, houses, roads
had once spread out from the central hub which is
now the ruined Hall. Once we started work we soon
found that where stone was not on the surface, it was
three inches down – or both. Even now if I plant a
small shrub in new ground a barrowload of stone has
to be taken out with a pickaxe before the shrub can
go in. The stone in the ground is one of the most
basic constraints of the garden, and I'm glad I was not
aware of it before we started. It can be very
discouraging. But now I see that it is the necessary
price to pay for the walls and the barns that create the
framework of the place and seem to gather the light
into themselves.

From the start I did have one incomparable asset in
my sister Pat, who is a horticulturalist. She has an
extraordinary sensitivity to both the biological and
aesthetic needs of plants, and knows how to use them
to their best advantage. Looking back at my first
attempts in the garden, I am surprised that she did not
throw up her hands in horror and walk away. But her
style is to apply the highest standards to her own
work, and the greatest tolerance to other people's. So
she has always guided and encouraged me, advising
me about cultivation and introducing me to new
forms and varieties of plants. Far from needing her
help less as I learn more, I find I need her weekend
advice increasingly as I get gradually more ambitious.

Hardly any of the ground was laid out as a garden, and
although there was huge scope for planting it was
clear that whole stretches between barns must be left
uncluttered by flowers or very cultivated shrubs. Even
the grass, out of which the stone barns rise directly,
would be out of keeping as a finely-mown lawn. It is
still cut to the length of a rough games pitch so that
the feeling of farmland remains distinct from the
garden itself. In fact, it was this distinction, as simple
as the decision on the cut of a sweep of grass, which
gave the clue to the style of the garden. The challenge
was to balance cultivation with the countryside, and
change with continuity. After all, a garden is not the
countryside, and cultivation is the human imprint on
the land. I write this retrospectively, and I am glad to
say that there was no such pompous or even
conscious thought in my mind at the time. I was
simply struggling along in a happy muddle. I was
aware of gratification if something began to fall into

place, and of dissatisfaction if something else did not.

I was searching for a definition, a style for the garden. I was also hunting for a single criterion, a word that I could work towards in this matter of style. Fortunately I did not want grandeur, which was not in the scale. Nor did I want formality, which was not in the shape. (Alas, no pleached limes for me.) What I did want above all was romance.

And what does that mean in a garden? It means old-fashioned roses falling out of apple trees. Dappled grass and secret places. Sentimental as you please. It means not rigid designs, not harsh colours, not regimented planting.

What else? How rash of me to have used the word in such a committed way about the style of my garden. My dictionary (and I only went to the Pocket Edition) offers a variety of definitions. I suppose I have the right to select or discard. Mainly it gives: preferring grandeur or picturesqueness or passion or irregular beauty, to finish or proportion. Picturesqueness I accept, and certainly passion and irregular beauty. But I see that I have already placed grandeur in actual opposition to my idea of romance, and I am sure that I strive endlessly to achieve even the most modest degree of finish and proportion.

And what about 'subordinating the whole to parts, or form to matter'? This is too confusing for me as applied to a garden, so I can only hope that the reference is intended as literary rather than horticultural, and leave it alone. 'Remote from ordinary life'? By all means if ordinary equates with dull. A last and unexpected throw from the Pocket Edition is: 'To draw the long bow.' How I wish I could find an excuse to use that phrase! It almost inspires me to turn the croquet pitch into an archery range.

Meanwhile a garden of any kind was still far into the future, and the first few years of hugely physical work were anything but romantic. Secateurs and hand trowels and green string, bought on the instant, lay neat and shiny and unused for a very long time. They are not the tools for demolition.

All through the first year I carted stone, burned nettle roots and generally cleaned up farm rubble. A few patches of clear ground were satisfying enough and there was time to watch and ponder as I clambered about. One fact established itself from the start: the farmer had gone and the livestock had gone (apart from one recidivist black hen who turned up plaintively and mysteriously from God knows where every weekend) but the place itself was still a farm. The strength of the house lay in centuries of informal working use, but its nature might very easily be destroyed by sophisticated or over-enthusiastic garden design or planting.

While the place was still being farmed, there were calves in the calf barn, old harness in the stables, and even hay in the tithe barn. Shown round by the friendly hard-working housekeeper I looked with more interest at the calves and the harness and the hay than at the barns and the sheds. Later, after the sale, when the dreaming had to stop and realism moved in, I admitted to a sinking feeling.

Empty farm buildings give out their own particular sense of desolation and uselessness and there were two particularly gloomy ones in the farmyard. One was for tractors, at right angles to the house, and the other, at the edge of the meadow, was a covered byre for milking. Both were open-fronted with heavy square beams holding up ugly bitumen roofs. We ripped off those roofs and found that we had gained a lot of sky and two arcades made of beams eight foot high and at right angles to others of the same length which were joined to freestanding walls. They were skeletons, bare and hard, but now expectant, waiting to be clothed, no longer old bones holding up depressing black coverings.

During all the hard labour I was longing to plant, watching to see what would grow and whether anything that appeared would be wanted or not. With some guilty feelings I scrapped a few things that were a perfectly reasonable part of the life of the previous farmer, but no good to me. For instance, in a patch of ground earmarked for a flowerbed, there appeared two powerful crowns of rhubarb. Poor rhubarb – we ate some young shoots and then dug the whole lot up. But a few plants appeared that had been perfectly chosen, and are still healthily and happily placed. The best is a pink cabbage-rose climbing all over the front of the house, not at all deterred by its due-north aspect. I think it is climbing 'Caroline Testout'. It flowers superbly in June and a bit more in August, and is hard work to dead-head from a ladder.

PAEONIA OFFICINALIS
One of the most confident flowers in the garden. The great scarlet heads and boldly-cut leaves announce summer whether the sun shines or not. My plants are more than twenty years old. I feed them every year with a rich compost but never disturb their roots. They are as vigorous as they were the first time that I saw them.

Another good legacy is a strong group of *Paeonia officinalis*, whose great scarlet mop heads and 'William Morris' leaves are the first herbaceous flowers to convince me that summer has really arrived. And the garden is blessed with an ample and recurrent supply of snowdrops and forget-me-nots which have probably grown there for years and years.

Having learnt a great deal about the tenacity of nettles, I next learnt a very small amount of lore about these forget-me-nots. While I was grubbing up some dead plants, a knowing countryman leaned over the churchyard wall to watch me, and said, 'Don't you like goldfinches in your garden then?'. I didn't know that goldfinches like forget-me-not seeds, but in any case I soon realised that the plants like to be left until they have seeded, so that in the autumn one can thin out next year's forget-me-not forest.

Being told about goldfinches in such a supercilious way quite dented my eagerness to learn country matters, but only briefly.

I knew that October and November were good months for planting, and made my first long lists of herbaceous plants and shrubs. I expected to spend a huge amount of money, and I was guided entirely by the principle of 'must have one of those', as I looked through the books. This principle does take you a few steps along the road, because you begin to recognise your own natural taste in plants. But once you have stuck them in the ground you are likely to find a most bewildering hotch-potch of mismatched favourites shooting up around you. That is, the ones that will decide to grow at all in your kind of soil.

I was saved from the very worst effects of this by a lucky stroke of ignorance. I went with my long lists to two or three of the garden centres with the very best reputations, and came home empty-handed and furious. 'But the books *say* plant in the autumn. Don't they *know* when to have the plants in?'

Eventually I realised that the great ally of garden centres is the spring. A damp autumn day does not entice people to go shopping for next year, browsing along rows of unattractively limp plants which are dying back for their winter rest (and which if unsold will probably die off completely, having once been lifted out of the ground). Whereas the first fine weekend of the year that brings the least hint of spring will tempt every gardener out of his house and every penny out of his pocket, and the garden centres are in business.

The fact is, I didn't even know about Nurseries and Orders. I hadn't joined the ranks of gardeners who can say, 'Where do you go for your shrubs?' or 'I found so-and-so's weren't up to much in my last order, but I found a few surprisingly good alpines in what's-his-name's last catalogue.'

Of course, this isn't really grand talk. In a really grand garden new plants are propagated under their own glass, and nurseries are only used for trees or bulbs or special varieties.

So I discovered about catalogues, as distinct from books, and lost the whole of the first planting season. This was desperately frustrating at the time, but probably a good thing with hindsight, as it gave me time to think about planning.

2

The Garden,

or Grubbing About in the Herbaceous Border

 ecause the garden covers so many separate places, there has been a problem of nomenclature. It is useless for me to say as I leave the house, 'If anyone wants me I'll be in the garden' because the garden spreads round three sides of the house and also round several corners. 'I'll be in the orchard' or 'I'll be behind the barn' is straightforward enough, but 'the garden' might mean half a dozen out-of-sight places. So the Garden, meaning the cultivated part, needs a separate name. 'I'll be in the Garden garden' is reasonable as a thought but a ridiculous thing to say. People think you are off to take the waters in Central Europe. More usefully, if more humbly, it tends to be 'the garden bit'.

Which means, as often as not, grubbing about in the herbaceous border.

In due course it became clear that the Garden part of the garden, with proper flowerbeds and lawn, would be on the north side of the house. There were already a couple of flowerbeds (the ones with the *Paeonia officinalis* and the forget-me-nots). Between them was a nearly square piece of grass surrounding five very old apple-trees while another patch of grass stretched away to the left. I settled this area of ground in my mind as the real garden, and there, in the shape of the old apple-trees, was my first ingredient for romance, ready-made and ancient indeed. For a year I took it for granted that the whole effect could hardly fail to be romantic, and then realised why I was so disappointed. Five apple-trees on a not very big lawn are a crowd. They obscured each other's lines and

gave no shape to the lawn either. It had not occurred
to me that an old tree might not necessarily be sacred,
but as soon as the unthinkable was thought, the
chain-saw demolished two of the trees in as many
days. At once we had three apple-trees, relaxed and
separate – almost romantic. It was the 'almost' that
made the next step obvious.

Between the house and the lawn lay a wide strip of
rather poor gravel. Long ago this must have been a
lane with the house standing right on it, with carts and
horses riding to the door and on through the
farmyard. The lane then became disused and gravel
must have been spread to tame it to garden
proportions. But cars were certainly not going to be
driven through *my* garden, and the wide strip of
gravel was ugly. I longed to have grass stretching all
the way across so that the house itself would rise out
of it. The relationship between stone and grass is
always cool and peaceful and very likely to be
romantic. So the drive was condemned although the
decision, unlike taking a chain-saw to the apple-trees,
was by no means no sooner said than done.

At around this time I came to recognise for the first
time the role that the Malcolms play in the garden. I
call them the Malcolms for the simple reason that they
are both called Malcolm. They are contract gardeners,
partners who turn up once a week and can tackle a
job like digging up gravel without a second thought.
When they first started working with me I was
thinking in terms of an occasional helping hand, a bit
of back-up if the work wasn't quite finished. It soon
became clear, however, that some of the physically
heavy projects would be well beyond my strength.
When we embark on one of these, the regular work of
mowing and spraying is shelved and the Malcolms
move in. They literally change the shape of the earth

for me – or the stone or the grass – by a combination of their talent for improvisation and their muscle power. Over the years the Malcolms have become an intrinsic part of the garden scene and in fact they are the scene-shifters.

Digging up a patch of gravel twelve by eighty feet, for instance, was a heavy, boring chore and extremely hard work, because the stony basis of it made real digging-over almost impossible. But the Malcolms tackled it and eventually the ground was sufficiently loosened to pour a load of good topsoil about three inches deep and then lay turf. Both house and garden were immediately enhanced.

These changes, disposing of trees and gravel, sound prosaic in their concept and their execution but at the same time they enabled me to start planting, actually putting into place some of my longed-for prerequisites for a romantic garden.

If you walk out of the big door of the house (I call it big because it is disproportionately large for the rest of the house and is very heavy and iron-studded) the apple-tree lawn and the west-facing herbaceous border are to your right. Straight in front of you along a stone path is the summerhouse. Halfway to the summerhouse the path ends in two shallowly-rising stone steps and beside them is the smallest and oldest of the apple-trees, a 'Beauty of Bath'. It was the first to be given a rose – 'Félicité et Perpétue', an old and vigorous rambler which spreads through every branch and tumbles out of the top in long sprays. The white flowers are tiny and flat, opening with a touch of pink into sprays of four or five many-petalled blooms on each stem, a distinctive formation I have not seen in any other rose. I believe it was named in the early nineteenth century for the daughters of the grower who, in their turn, were named for two girls who were thrown to the lions at Carthage and subsequently canonised as St Felicitas and St Perpetua. They, or rather it, only needs light pruning or an occasional old shoot cut out from the base. It blooms towards the end of July, a late *bonne-bouche* when most of the old roses are finished.

Beside the stone step, and of very low growth but just reaching up to the lowest branches of the same apple-tree, is a 'Raubritter' rose, a small shrub of Macrantha origin. Its bright pink blooms are cupped in a rounded chubby way which gives it a childish look. In fact I think of both of these as children's roses. Even the 'Beauty of Bath' apples are small, like the rough red cheeks of a healthy, chubby urchin.

On towards the summerhouse. Mine is not the only summerhouse to have started as a loo, I am sure. Ours must have been built by a farmer who believed in togetherness, because it was furnished only with a strong plank with three neat round holes cut in it. The remains of a rough path of stone and ash led away from it in a shallow curve, and after about ten yards petered out into the lawn. For some five years I left it severely alone, half-hidden, dank and forlorn under a huge sycamore.

One day I realised that the shade and the drips from the sycamore were ruining a very large patch of potentially good garden. After much heart-searching we took a deep breath and had it cut down. Immediately the garden lightened and looked cheerful, and the little family loo was exposed as a distinct 'feature'. It was facing south and clearly laid claim to be the summerhouse. It needed only a good

scrub and a minimum of patching and pointing
before I could plant.

On its left I put a *Clematis spooneri*, intended to
scramble over both the sycamore stump and one side
of the little house, and on its right a large-flowered
double white clematis, the 'Duchess of Edinburgh',
and *Solanum jasminoides* 'Album'. I try to drape the
'Duchess', which is extremely strong, across the
solanum before it dies back in winter because the
solanum is very tender. Two years ago I thought I had
lost it, after a long and hard frost, and although it
eventually came back it started so late that
maddeningly it only made a lot of leaf and was too
late to flower. It is one of the most beautiful and
delicate of climbers with its white sprays of flowers,
gold-stamened, standing well out from the stems and
giving it a very airy look. Ten times better to my mind,
though much less serviceable and hardy, than the
ordinary blue solanum. There is a good blue variety
called 'Glasnevin' but it is still unmistakably a
climbing potato plant.

The *Clematis spooneri*, which is really *Clematis
chrysocoma sericea*, is like a rather opulent version of
a white *montana*, but slightly broader-petalled. In its
first year every one of its plentiful shoots was nibbled
off, day after day. I never discovered whether its
enemies were mice, squirrels or pigeons, but now
that the plant is a little older and presumably tougher,
it is evidently not such a delicacy. It has had a chance
to establish itself and perhaps mistook the attacks
upon it for pruning, because it is now flowering
massively. At first I tried some complicated protective
plastic netting but this only made the nibbling worse,
as though I had provided a helpful climbing frame, a
sort of adventure playground for whole families of
little predators.

The stony path that leads away from the summerhouse is on a downhill slope, and as there is no rockery in the garden it makes a good site for alpines. I find it difficult to visualise or even to believe in the size that an alpine wants to grow when I buy a tiny speck in a pot, so the planting changes from year to year as a phlox sprawls or a pink retreats. And there are always little starry things to be found in nurseries which are irresistible, but which don't always survive. Small bulbs – *Iris histrioides* and *Narcissus minimus* – get the alpine steps off to a good early start, and last year I put in what appears to be the smallest campanula in the world. It is severely named 'E. J. Toogood' but I have not yet discovered which of the impressively-named diminutive sub-species it belongs to.

SUMMERHOUSE WITH JOAN OF ARC
Whoever built this went to considerable trouble to put a pyramidally tiled roof above well-faced stone, to construct a lavatory for the farmer's family. The proportions seem right for our stone Joan of Arc who kneels with her helmet beside her. She is battered, and she has lost her sword. I know nothing of her provenance, other than that she is French.

We talk about the summerhouse, and we talk about the alpine steps, but I still think of it as a crummy little loo and its loo path. I see that my dictionary definitions of romance do not include plastic netting, or lavatories, or even 'E. J. Toogood', but it is nevertheless very romantic.

The herbaceous border is west-facing, that is to say, on the right-hand side of the apple-tree lawn as you come out of the big door. So it is at right-angles to the house, about seven feet deep and fifty feet long, backed by a wall. The near end of the wall is covered by a 'New Dawn' rose whose soft double blooms spread about in a relaxed way with hardly any support. It gradually set the theme for the herbaceous border and has now come to dominate it. Its sprays dip delicately over and into the plants in front of it so that pale pink rules. OK by me. Under the 'New Dawn' is an ordinary catmint, long-flowering and loosely spreading, and in front of that, among the mid-border plants, are some *Euphorbia epithymoides*. They make neat clumps, brilliantly lime-yellow, and as they flower in late spring they accompany the last of the bulbs, helping the transition into early summer which can be a bit colourless and discouraging for a week or two. If these euphorbias are cut right down as soon as they have finished flowering, one loses a month of good green leaf but gains a second flowering in July. Then they coincide with the 'New Dawn' itself, making a bright clear contrast to it, the catmint and the shades of pinks and purples in the border. (The catmint meanwhile has grown up fast and conveniently in early June to hide the dying leaves of late daffodils behind it.)

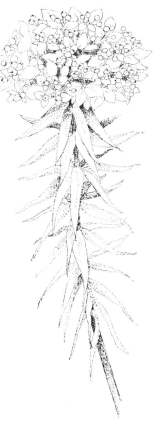

EUPHORBIA EPITHYMOIDES
This plant is synonymous with E. polychroma. *It makes tidy clumps that are easily divided and its bracts are a brilliant lime-green. They stand neatly above fresh green leaves and associate well with the yellows and pinks of late spring in the border.*

Beyond the 'New Dawn' and well to the back are *Echinops ritro* and *Verbascum* 'Domino'. Both of them are powerful and heavy plants making a strong background against which others can look light. On the whole I favour tall, spiky and feathery shapes in the herbaceous border to keep the texture as light as I possibly can. Nothing, for instance, can be more feathery and airy than a bronze fennel. It also has the interesting though sometimes exasperating habit of moving about. That is, it is not very long-lived and its root may rot in winter, but seedlings have meanwhile appeared elsewhere, and these can easily reach their mature three to four feet in one season. It is a matter of choosing the best-placed seedlings in relation to their neighbouring plants and scrapping the rest. They don't transplant easily except when they are extremely young because they send down a long tap-root within weeks of germinating. One has to keep a sharp lookout because they are very inconspicuous as babies, and by the time they are noticed they may be hard to lift.

Gypsophila here and there in the mid-border and *Alchemilla mollis* towards the front are both useful and well-known lighteners. It is well worth cutting alchemilla right down as soon as the flowers begin to go brown and floppy. High summer is a bad time for it, but little fresh leaves appear and grow fast when the first heavy growth is cut away.

Also at the back, past the echinops and in apple-tree shade is a stretch of Solomon's seal which appears with steadfast promise every April and never fails to be elegant and shapely. Among the more solid forms that anchor the border are a couple of late single paeonies, both of them pale and more rounded than the more vigorous ones. They are called 'White Wings' and 'Globe of Light'. They contrast with the tall sprays and spikes without being too heavy themselves.

What next? Some geraniums, various campanulas, some pinks, some pansies and violas, a few irises – what use are lists except for the long winter evenings.

I suppose the placing and the timing are two of the secrets of border-making. With determination and pencil and paper I am sure that I could exploit these crucial factors to great advantage. Somehow in my case it very frequently happens that the two plants that would complement each other best happen to live at opposite ends of the garden. Whereas, conversely, one perfectly good plant defeats another in either colour or form simply by their too close proximity. Lately I was greatly taken by a thalictrum which I saw floating prettily above close-leaved paeonies and against a dark hedge of holly. I bought two beautiful varieties *T. aquilegifolium* and *T. dipterocarpum*, found a gap and stuck them in. They came up delicately but were totally invisible in front of a light-blue veronica at the height of its season.

Dark backgrounds are a great asset in a garden, and I suffer from a complete lack of them. For instance, I also planted a *Clematis flammula* which I had seen in a friend's garden. It was shown off there in a profusion of brilliant white stars scrambling (I know stars don't scramble but clematis does) over a dark laurel. My *flammula* has only a Cotswold wall behind it and is insignificant without the contrast. I rationalise my mistake by trying to think of it as subtle, something special that you have to look for, but in fact it is a failure. Incidentally, a great advantage to *Clematis flammula* is that it flowers all through September and October.

So much for placing, but I am not yet out of the wood because one of the hardest lessons in border planting is the timing. I have had inspired thoughts about associations of plants only to find, after months of anticipation, that one flower is going over just as its artistically-placed neighbour is opening its first bud. Then I grow despondent and wonder if the compatibilities of colour and shape and scale can ever be caught when there are so many variables to contend with. But there are common denominators too, and certain simple preferences more instinctive than any conscious sense of taste or design seem to ensure a general harmony in planting.

For the most part, by the middle of May one's eye is grateful for the abundant growing, the filling-up, the unfurling and the promise, so that criticism and dissatisfactions are kept at bay for a while. From then on the border itself takes over as the season develops through June and July.

May, superb as it is, is not the month for romance. It is too eager, too fast-moving, and the shoots are too straight and strong. Early bees rush about, hard-working birds shout at each other and there is a sense of vigorous achievement on every side. Even April, with its tentative spring flowers, is more romantic than May.

Longing for June, hating to lose May, I expend a great deal of nervous energy waiting for the old-fashioned roses, whose arrival I cannot of course influence by a single day. Their home is in the left-hand half of the garden as you walk, yet again, out of the big door of the house. It is the squarish patch of ground that is continuous with the apple-tree lawn on one side and bounded by a five-foot wall round the other three sides. It was rough grass when we arrived. I think it had been used for vegetables once because it is quite near to the house, sheltered and out of range of passing livestock who might help themselves to a cabbage or munch up a few lettuces on their way to or from milking or pasture. It was in any case less stony than most of the land, and easier to dig over.

I cleared a patch, made three holes and popped in three old-fashioned roses with the most romantic names I could think of: 'Fantin Latour', the old shrub rose named for the French painter; 'Souvenir de la Malmaison', a pale Bourbon rose, and *Rosa × alba*, the 'White Rose of York'. They looked rather forlorn little shrubs with their pathetic bare circles cut out of the long grass, and up to their ears in muck. The 'Souvenir' died after a reluctant year or two of struggling against mildew and black spot. It is not an easy rose.

I turned my attention from the other two and began planting. There was space here and I could indulge in 'must-have-one-of-those'. Before long a silver birch was making its way upwards in front of a few different hollies in one corner, with a pretty *Robinia kelseyi* in the other. This has delightful pink flowers in June, hanging in racemes like a frail wisteria. There is an extraordinary brittleness about robinia when young, and branches may crack right off in high winds, so it needs to be sheltered. Twice in its second year I found branches torn as though it had been vandalised, but it seems tougher and more secure now, at six years old.

I added in a lilac, a tree paeony (the common one called *Paeonia lutea ludlowii* with its strange and magnificently cut leaves) and its cousin the bush poppy, *Romneya coulteri*. This is a bit tender and

ROBINIA KELSEYI
This is an elegant tree. It has the classical top-heavy acacia shape, and the pinnate leaves, but does not grow taller than ten feet whereas the common pseudoacacia *reaches thirty feet. It bears soft pink flowers which hang in racemes not unlike a smaller version of wisteria and is one of the prettiest flowering trees. It needs a sheltered spot, as its boughs may actually be torn off or cracked in a high wind.*

during its first winter I remembered it late one snowy
night and rushed out to wrap a towel round its roots.
It was unsuitable protection and I felt a fool, but it
worked and now it is a large grey-green plant that
grows up completely from ground level each year. It
bears a succession of flowers through July and August
that look like huge poached eggs made of crinkly
taffeta silk.

While 'Fantin Latour' and *Rosa × alba* began to
thrive, my rose garden had somehow been forgotten.
I began to go through the lists of roses, and my head
was soon reeling with the names and the
descriptions. Even the rose families' names are
beautiful and evocative of their distant origins – the
Damasks and the *gallicas*, the Musks and the China
roses. The catalogues dealt in superlatives and
although I believed in them implicitly, I forced myself
to look for trouble in the more objective gardening
books.

   After much inner debate I bought about ten roses.
The planting, however, remained totally haphazard.
(Even Pat could not really teach me not to overplant:
that is a lesson in patience that each enthusiastic
beginner has to learn the hard way and with
hindsight, when crowded plants start to struggle for
space as they grow.)

   I suppose that because there was plenty of space I
had some notion of a 'sweet disorder', but the result
was a nonsensical muddle with some beautiful young
roses dotted aimlessly about. The situation was
eventually saved by my husband Peter. As usual he
had not interfered with my planting, but after a while
he said gently, 'What is the point here, exactly?' often

enough for me to realise that the exercise was in fact
without point, a vague self-indulgence.

Fortunately most of the other planting was round
the edge, because the idea that gradually came into
focus was to make a circle of the old-fashioned roses.
That winter we planned and moved and planted all
over again. The roses have very different habits and
characters and the question of who should go beside
whom needed to be settled. With another ten roses
bought and one or two banished, the full
complement is now twenty-one including two little
'Rosa Mundi', one on each side of the gap that leads
into the circle which is about twenty yards across.

I try to keep to my own rule of planting with all of
them, which is that they each should have their own
complete space. One or two do overlap because I
have underrated their capacity and planted them too
closely, but they are not improved by it. There is a
sense of serenity and dignity in old roses
freestanding in grass, that is quite lost if they are
jumbled together in a clump. By the same token those
roses are usually wasted and uncomfortable in flower
beds.

'Fantin Latour' became and has remained the key
note. It is hard to choose between the others but my
three favourites dominate the rest. One is 'Gypsy Boy'
or 'Zigeunerknabe', a deep crimson Bourbon whose
clusters fade to a dusty purple as they age. This is
actually 'Son of Gypsy Boy' because it is my own
cutting from the rose on the terrace. I am proud and
parental about it because I don't often succeed with
roses from cuttings. 'Gypsy Boy' is a good one to
practise on because it is such a vigorous plant and
easy to propagate. The second of my trio is 'Celsiana',
the prettiest possible pink Damask rose, slightly frilly,
semi-double with bright gold stamens. I could hardly

believe it would survive uprooting at four years old but I cut it almost to the ground and it was flowering perfectly happily the next summer. The third is the 'Queen of Denmark' ('Königin von Dänemark'), a big Alba rose, fully quartered and a clear pink. It looks a really classic old-fashioned rose, though I believe it is not in fact of very ancient origin.

Beside the rose circle, but not part of it, I have planted an 'Apothecary's Rose', the *Rosa gallica* 'Officinalis'. It has a simple bright pink flower and you might not choose it for its looks. I first saw it at the Chelsea Physic Garden and only then discovered that it is the true ancestor of every rose in my garden, whether old or new, so it stands outside the circle as an honourable forbear.

Now there is a plain birdbath in the centre of the circle, and we mow the grass shorter inside the roses to accentuate the symmetry. But there is one other inhabitant which is, I am sorry to say, a *Viburnum tomentosum* 'Lanarth'. I planted it long before the roses and it is well off-centre. Fortunately it has finished its flowering season before the roses start, so it is less conspicuous in the rose season. It looks grand and established now, settled firmly and creamily into its wide skirts, and it has no intention of moving.

The rest of the garden bit is across the front of the house. The planting of this is determined by practicalities because, facing due north as it does, it is completely without sun. However, the ground is fairly damp and the prevailing wind drives the rain against that side of the house. Damp shade seems to be an easier proposition than dry shade, and I have been surprised at the variety of plants that I have been able to persuade to thrive along that wall. I wonder whether a faint warmth penetrates from the inside of the house so that in the coldest weeks of winter, it is fractionally milder there. I intend to compare the temperatures in this part of the garden with another northerly wall away from the house. The windows of three rooms face from the north side of the house – the kitchen, the dining room and the sitting room.

The kitchen window has a 'Royal Velours' clematis and an 'Altissimo' rose growing round it. They both flower in late summer, when their strong colours are welcome. The clematis is a deep velvety purple, very simple with four formal petals, and the rose is also a simply-shaped flower of a very deep red. Together they intertwine in a rather heraldic fashion.

Beneath them under the kitchen window is a bed of *Helleborus orientalis*. These are wonderful in early spring, often hit hard by late frosts but always resilient, and flowering for weeks and weeks. Since

HELLEBORUS ORIENTALIS
Their dark reds, dusky pinks and pure whites all have distinctive and individual markings inside the flower. Books and catalogues usually describe them only as 'variable'. I would call them exquisite, romantic and without equal.

they never come quite true from seed, slightly
different markings and colourings appear from one
plant to another. The fun is to collect more and more
varieties of these beautiful hellebores. For all the
pinks and reds, and with even a lovely and quite rare
butter-yellow, my favourites are always the white
ones, some with greenish markings inside the petals,
some with red. They are very hardy, and will grow in
total shade, but nearly always wilt as soon as they are
picked. When I feel I must bring one or two into the
house I take a jug of water out to them and cut them
straight into it. Then they sit on a shelf high up in the
room so that for once I can look straight into their
faces, instead of having to lie flat on the ground and
tip them up.

   The middle third of the house is taken up by the
dining-room window. On one side of it is a *Cytisus
battandieri*, and on the other a 'Mermaid' rose
(*must*-have-one-of-those). It is possible that the
'Mermaid' would be the better for the odd shaft of
sunlight, but it is surprising how easily the cytisus
accepts its north aspect. The yellow pineapple-
scented flowers are large and profuse and the leaves
remain a silky silver-green all through the season.
Under the window I have planted a little evergreen
hedge of rue whose colour is a shade deeper and
more blue than the cytisus but which tones in with it
very well. Unfortunately I find its smell so repellent
that I have to hold my breath when I touch it, which I
only do in order to cut off its boring little yellow
flowers. But it looks attractive against the stone wall
and there are not many plants which would thrive
there. Rosemary and lavender would never tolerate
that position, but the rue looks quite happy.

   Finally, the drawing-room window. This is
separated from the dining room by the big door and

CYTISUS BATTANDIERI
*This climber does not mind
being trained closely to a
wall and is hardier than it
looks. Its silvery leaves keep
their silky texture for the
whole season so that the
plant looks fresh even in late
summer. The complicated
flowers, like an upside-down
laburnum, are a strong
clear yellow and have a
delicious scent of pineapple.*

the porch and outside it there was once a small dairy built as a lean-to to the house. It must have been cool and dark, and now only the stone-flagged floor remains, a couple of steps down from the garden level. The corners, and the places where the stones are broken, are ideal crevices for hostas and ferns and a few more hellebores. The little dark *Helleborus atrorubens*, a frilly *H. foetidus* and a few more *H. orientalis* flourish there, although the Christmas rose, *H. niger*, snowy and pure in other people's gardens, arrives for me in late spring, always muddy and usually chewed by mice.

Against the wall is a dark *Hydrangea petiolaris* and with some of the stones mossy, some bare, the whole impression is of shades of green and grey with a few points of subdued colour from a patch of red astrantia and another of the tall *Geranium phaeum* called the 'Widow'. The moment when the ferns and hostas reappear in early May is a lovely time to see them because they unfurl so appealingly.

Rising from the floor, high above the little dairy corner is our inherited 'Caroline Testout' flowering right up the house, a real old country rose. It is also surprisingly happy without sun, and round its feet is a clump of epimedium, a useful spreader with prettily marked foliage, which I think of as a cheery little plant because my mother used to call it Happy Medium.

Most climbing plants seem to need plenty of light, even if not direct sunlight and this is probably why the 'Caroline Testout' rose and the *Cytisus battandieri* are both rather leggy, with few branches near the ground. They become better furnished as they grow taller, evidently searching for the lighter air. Their pruning and tying-in become, as a result, both inconvenient and precarious.

Across the way from the dairy garden is the original

flowerbed that predates our arrival and is called the pump bed. There is in fact a deep well in the middle of it, surrounded by a low stone wall with a rusty old pump standing four feet high out of it. You can hear water running into the well from the water table nearly all the year round. Here are the big red double paeonies, and they still have pride of place among the strong plants and colours that fill the bed. Delphiniums and lupins, a philadelphus and tall white daisies being equally dominant can let fly here without threatening each other. It is a cheerful summer bed, and yet my least favourite. There are always a few blank patches in it, and two wicked perennial weeds, a convolvulus and a wild campanula against which I do constant battle, never winning.

The pump itself is blue-tit territory, and inside it is the safest nest in the garden. Once the eggs hatch you can shade your eyes, peer down the four-inch wide cylinder, and see straight into five or six little gaping throats which stretch up as your shadow crosses them. If the mother is sitting, she will spit and fluff up bravely against your intrusion. I have not solved the mystery of the young birds' very first flight which must be a four-foot vertical take-off, but they always seem to manage.

One day a lady came to the gate and asked if she might show her children the place, as she herself had spent childhood holidays on the farm years ago. As we walked round, she remembered playing hide and seek in the barns, and jumping into the hay to chase the chickens. When we passed the pump she said, 'Oh, I had forgotten that old pump. Look children, blue tits used to nest inside that every year.' And an obliging blue tit immediately arrived with its lilting flight, a grub in its beak, and hopped into the pump. I believe she thought it was a ghost.

One last separate entity between the pump bed and
the summerhouse is a *subhirtella*, the winter
flowering prunus. Its starry little white flowers come
out beautifully in December but quickly get
wretchedly frosted. They will vanish all through the
hard weather, to appear again after the frosts with
pink flowers in late March and April. Under the little
tree the dog-toothed violets, only six inches high, are
also April flowering. They are in fact bulbs which
make small clumps, and are quite undemanding like
most other bulbs. Mine are the creamy *Erythronium
dens-canis* 'White Splendour'. Having withstood some
destructive nibbling from squirrels when I first
planted them, they are now well established. They do

ERYTHRONIUM DENS-CANIS
*The delicately poised flowers
with their subtle creamy
petals and dark red
markings make them look
tender and exotic. They are
in fact quite hardy and easy
to cultivate, once their little
bulbs have established.*

not remind me of dogs or teeth or violets. Each one
rises delicately above a patterned rosette of leaves,
facing towards the ground with its petals curved
backwards. They have a small and stately look under
the *subhirtella*, so difficult to describe. I cannot think
of another flower that is so beautiful although it is
only seen from the back. It was only by luck that I
chose to plant mine in a very open place so that the
light shines through them both morning and evening.

It has not always been necessary to give every part of
the garden an identity. There is one place in fact
where nothing happens at all. Nothing is growing in it
except grass, there is nothing to do and nowhere
even to sit. It is not reasonable to think of one piece of
ground as older than another but perhaps it has
served the same purpose for a very long time, so that
gives it a claim to be the oldest part of the garden.

Yet as I have said it is not garden. It is the place
behind the tithe barn. Less than half an acre and
nearly square, it is walled on three sides. Its fourth
side, on the west, is the back wall of the tithe barn
which is itself probably older than any of the ruins
still standing, and may be, with its small pre-Norman
buttresses, a remaining part of the original Minster.
The shallow flight of steps from the lower pool leads
down into it for no particular reason except that the
slope would be steep without steps. Like the
neighbouring sunken garden, it is at a low level,
which makes it sheltered. Two huge pairs of massive
double doors in the barn open into it, so that a
hayload could have been driven in from the fields, or
corn for threshing. In more recent times cattle stood
there before milking, but there is no feeling of activity

about the place now. The actual silence is accentuated by its unusual stillness, since there is nothing to look at, or at least nothing that changes.

In our first few years of the garden I used to tinker with ideas about putting it to one use or another. A few trees? Shrubs? An enclosed vegetable garden? Perhaps through laziness I followed none of these plans. There was then, as there always will be, more than enough to do. But it was not laziness. The character of the place resisted my interference, and thank goodness it won. However absorbing the pleasure and interest in the rest of the garden, the empty place behind the tithe barn, which is old and silent, is sometimes the best place to be. It hasn't even got a name.

3

The Orchard and its Terrace,

or Taking Out a Hole

 imagine that where there is an orchard in a garden it has usually pre-existed the owner: few people now seem to feel compelled to plant one. It had certainly not even crossed my mind as a necessary part of a garden although I would have welcomed a ready-made one. I suppose the old apple-trees on the lawn were left over from an erstwhile orchard but their fruit, though still prolific, is incidental. In a sense this is also the case with our young orchard because I planted it primarily for the sake of the design of the garden as a whole, so the fruit is a bonus.

The orchard began life as a piece of rough ground covered with disused concrete pigsties. These had to be grubbed up and removed by a man with a machine. We sowed grass seed and soon found ourselves with a good clear stretch of land, nearly half an acre, between the house and the Ruins. Over its west wall lay the churchyard, and the tithe barn was off to the east over another low wall. Our own view of the Ruins was reciprocated by the very clear view that every passing tourist had of us. The dividing wall is just the right height to tempt people to peer over and it was not long before we felt the lack of privacy. To have raised the wall would have been extremely expensive and anyway impracticable. Trees would eventually have grown to a height which would have hidden the Ruins but would still have left space between their trunks for tourists to continue their scrutiny. By which time we would have been too old to care anyway. Or even dead.

Her years in Kent and her expertise with apple-trees brought the answer immediately to Pat's mind. Standing at the kitchen window my sister took one look across the new grass and said, 'That's the orchard'. It was clearly the only possible solution.

She sent me not only a list of trees to order but a plan of their planting in relation to each other. I later found out that everything about her choice of trees had a good reason, so for once I learnt the easy way.

I ordered them all as dwarfing rootstock from Scott's at Merriott in Somerset and one mild January weekend the eleven bare twiggy young trees were planted. Dwarfing rootstock sounded unromantic, but usefully meant that the grown trees would be between ten and twelve feet in both height and width and the branches would start low from the ground.

With as many fruit trees as I needed and could look after, but only just enough to dignify their home with the name of orchard, the shape of their planting as well as their relative proximity needed planning. A straight line had little to commend it, and groups of trees planted over the whole of the available area would not only occupy an unnecessary amount of space but not be effective as a screen. After much thought and standing about trying to look like apple-trees we decided on one double row of trees in a gentle crescent shape, leaving quite a large lawn in front of them. To accentuate this crescent shape and the identity of the orchard, I keep the lawn grass short in front of the trees following the curved line. Behind that line the trees themselves stand in grass of a slightly longer fortnightly cut. It was the first time I tried this simple device. I have used it more than once since then: it helps the eye to discern areas of different character.

From the beginning my fruit trees were all healthy little fellows, taking up nice open shapes without trouble. Now maturing, they are not only the best size and shape for picking the fruit and reaching the boughs for pruning, but they also make an informal screen along the side of the Ruins at just the right height.

When they were about three years old, the first few apples appeared and there was much clucking approval from the family as if at a child's early achievements. The pears were backward by comparison, so they were ignored. In their fifth year the apple-trees themselves began to take on different characteristics and shapes, and from then on there have been real crops of apples, all wonderfully different.

None of this happy fertility, I found, owed anything to chance, but was due to Pat's choice of varieties, and her choice was itself determined by the times of blossoming. I had never appreciated this factor before, Apple Blossom Time being for me one glorious, though short, fact of life. But it seems that most fruit trees like to be fertilised by other varieties, though most of them are not fussy about which. So one chooses varieties whose blooms open at the same time and plants them within flirting distance of each other. In the case of dwarfing trees this is about fifteen feet apart. In my orchard there are 'James Grieve', 'Lord Lambourne' and 'Tydeman's Late Orange' within range of one another, then 'Annie Elizabeth' and 'Grenadier'. Next come four pears, 'Fondante d'Automne' and 'Gorham', then 'Conference' and 'Doyenné du Comice'. At the end of the line is a later addition, an old apple called 'Ashmead's Kernel'. It has a wonderful flavour and crispness and appears not to mind that its neighbours are pear-trees because it already has plenty of apples in its fourth year.

The pear-trees need patience over the matter of fruit. I kept reminding myself that they were not

planted for the fruit, but it cannot but be frustrating to
see every pear being stolen by various forms of
wildlife before they are ready to pick. Blackbirds peck
at the fruit just beside the stalk so that they rot and fall
off. Wasps besiege them and leave hollow skins. Last
year I saw a squirrel sitting up in a pile of the best
pears that he had assembled, holding one in his front
paws while he nibbled and munched at top speed.
Articles in autumn gardening columns earnestly
recommend one to tie little bags round each pear
before it is attacked but I know that I could never
aspire to such perfectionism. I employ the other form
of patience, which is to wait, eating the greengrocer's
pears meanwhile. This has paid off because now, in a
good year, there is enough fruit for the birds and the
wasps to take their fill and still leave a small crop for
me and the squirrels.

Planting, particularly of the trees in the orchard,
taught me one of my early phrases of gardening
jargon. That is, you never dig a hole. You take out a
hole. If trees are going in, I was told by a friend who is
a 'serious gardener', be sure you take out big enough
holes, and take them out ahead of time. You need to
put in the manure and so on a couple of weeks
before, and you don't want to be caught short with
your bare rootstock arriving and your holes not taken
out. No indeed. I was quite shocked, as well as
impressed, by the very idea of all that and started right
away. Now I say it as a matter of course, but it did
sound wonderfully affected at first.

  But whether I dig a hole or take it out, I believe that
my worst disappointments and setbacks in the garden
have been caused by not making planting holes big

enough. In very stony ground such as mine, the
temptation is to stop short and hope for the best. But
time and again this has led to my losing plants,
particularly shrubs. At best they have started slowly,
taking years to get their roots down and grow well.
(To grow well is an extremely amateurish thing to say.
I should have said 'to go away'. It is very smart to
stand back from a young shrub you have just planted
and fed and watered and generally tucked up nicely,
and say, 'There, I think that should go away quite well
now.' It can be rather disconcerting to the
uninitiated.)

I now take this question of planting very seriously,
so much so that I embark on it with a pickaxe as well
as a spade, and if possible a husband too. The
corollary to the barrows of stone that get carted away
in the course of planting is that extra earth then needs
to be brought in. After loosening the sides of the hole
as well as the bottom and putting in a layer of muck
followed by some wet peat and a handful of
bonemeal, I still find myself short of earth for my new
plant. This is the one blessing provided by otherwise
cursed moles. Their beastly hills are a source of finely
sieved loam which I store in various corners and can
then use as ideally worked earth to give young roots a
start.

The need for adequate planting and then for constant
watering in the following year have been costly
lessons for me to learn in time as well as in money.
Say you have a bright idea one spring day for the
exact shrub you need for a particular corner. It might
be a ceanothus and a variety that is slightly tender but
not desperately so. You order it; by the late autumn it

arrives, and you plant it. There are a thousand other jobs to do that week and it gets planted in something of a hurry. With luck it has time to establish itself a little bit before the winter sets in, and may be off to a slightly quicker start in the spring. Without luck, it gets badly knocked back by the cold weather and you wish you had waited till spring before planting it. Either way it is only a tiddler that first season, fun to watch but nowhere near to making its contribution.

In the following year it may put out a few flowering shoots. This is progress and you feel a sense of pleasant impatience. By this time it wants to grow fast in late summer and is big enough to come up against the edges of your hole. Which you didn't take out quite deep enough or wide enough, so the fine ends of roots meet stone. They push and twist and double back, searching for a way round, but being a bit dry (it being the only fine August for years, you have been lying on the lawn instead of watering) they are not very supple. They begin to shrivel, and the tips are frayed. You can't see this, but next season it is clear that your ceanothus has not come through the winter very well. In fact it has very little more to offer than last year. You cosset it with plenty of feeding of various kinds and hope for the best. But the following winter is a really hard long one, and by the time spring comes again you may feel that it is not really worth keeping for the sake of the only two surviving shoots.

You can't order another till next autumn. Five years can easily pass before your original idea is even beginning to be a reality. One can go off the most brilliant of ideas in that length of time. Of course there may have been all kinds of other hazards to challenge your poor, not-very-hardy ceanothus, but one thing is certain. The second time round you find the energy to carry buckets of water to it, and you take out a very big hole.

Planting difficulties in the orchard are well behind us now and other problems appear unexpectedly in the usually well-behaved and now sizeable trees. In its sixth year, the central apple, 'Tydeman's Late Orange' suddenly decided to grow more vigorously than its fellows and shot up, threatening to become unreachable and disproportionate, forgetting its title of dwarf tree. That winter, after a good crop of apples and after its leaves had fallen, I pruned it hard, down to the spurs. That is, I cut off each of the year's side shoots to within a mere knuckle of the previous year's growth, and shortened each leader (the single main shoot of every big branch) by at least a half. With variations that is standard practice for winter pruning of apple-trees, and I was beginning to get the hang of it. But that was not all. I then, with great determination, sawed out the centre of the tree to my own shoulder height, hoping to keep the total size and shape within bounds. 'Bounds', for my purpose, means being able to reach the fruit without climbing up a ladder, and not allowing the trees to reach a height which obscures the Ruins or our view towards the river. 'Tydeman's Late Orange' responded in its own vigorous way: the following year there were practically no apples, but all the new shoots, of which there were hundreds, raced straight upwards to a height of at least four foot from their parent boughs. By midsummer the tree was a vast chandelier, towering over its neighbours, because by cutting out the centre I had forced the growth into the side branches. Pat was called in for consultation, and her

advice was to summer prune sternly. This meant
shortening each new shoot to about four leaves –
quite a simple hour's work with the secateurs, the
principle being to check the whole tree while it was
still growing fast in July and August. Winter pruning
was then as usual, a repeat performance down to the
spur. The whole tree still kept a good shape because
the centre had been removed, and the operation
turned out to be a success.

I now keep a close eye on the orchard's summer
growth. After any particularly hard pruning or
shaping in a previous winter I prowl between the
trees, snapping my secateurs menacingly and peering
at the shoots, ready to summer prune if any of them
threatens to get out of line.

The furthest tree in the orchard crescent is a crab-
apple. These are completely different from other
apples, being ornamental maluses, so they are not
grafted as dwarfing shrubs like the others. Mine is a
'John Downie', small and narrow and growing in a
disciplined upright way, with particularly bright

MALUS 'JOHN DOWNIE'
The clear white of the
blossom and the clear red of
the small crab-apples give
'John Downie' the
personality of two
completely different trees
every year.

blossom and masses of enchanting little scarlet crab-apples all along each bough. I have never touched it with secateurs and it looks after itself neatly. As I never bother to make crab-apple jelly I am only interested in its looks and its shape, and these have never needed my interference.

However, one hard winter ice got inside its trunk and burst the bark. By the time I noticed it, the bark had dried and contracted so that it could no longer meet round the trunk. The split was four feet long, almost the full length of the tree before it branched, and I could have simply lifted the bark off all the way round. I knew that no tree could survive this degree of detachment of its bark, so I bound it back on as firmly as I could with two pairs of tights as bandages, and hoped that it might heal. In the spring the tree blossomed, although poorly, and as soon as the leaves came they began to fall at the same time as the dead blossom. By June there was no fruit on the tree and very few leaves. Those that remained had a dusty blackish look and I wondered with dread how to recognise honey fungus, imagining that every tree in the orchard would have to be burned. I dared not show it to Pat for fear of her verdict. Fortunately I forgot about it for a while, probably encouraged by the ostrich who lives in my subconscious mind. The next year it was just a little healthier after a strong winterfeed of manure. In the summer, however, the fruits fell off again and I thought that the tights, which are surprisingly strong and which I often use as tree ties or bandages, might be constricting the bond which must have been forming between the trunk and the bark.

(At last I could acknowledge a practical application of my expensive education. On a fifth form blackboard there had been one diagram that I had never forgotten, a sort of scaffolding inside the bark of a tree. Tiny nutritive particles whizzed up the scaffolding in one direction, and other particles dashed down in the opposite direction.)

I cut off the tights, so as not to obstruct this essential whizzing up and dashing down. The bark was secure again, apart from a nearly-healed scar where it could not quite meet round the trunk. The next season 'John Downie' was restored even to the little red apples. Thanks possibly to my botany mistress who had imbued in me a childish picture of a tree's metabolic needs.

A garden like mine can look very haphazard if the planting becomes indiscriminate, and my desire for more and more plants would soon overrule my sense of design if I were left to myself. I can see now how often Peter's more disciplined eye has saved me from creating an impression of Greater Spotted Chaos.

Against the low wall bounding the east side of the orchard I planted a *rubrifolia* rose, which I remembered from my mother's garden. By lucky chance I had placed it where its blue leaves and pink flowers, (and later hips), caught the low evening sunshine when the sprays were beautifully lit. When I first saw this effect on the then small plant, my reaction was, 'How lovely! What else can we think of to put along that wall?' Peter's reaction was, 'How lovely. Let's have *rubrifolia* along its whole length.' It is now the *rubrifolia* wall and for a stretch of twenty yards, there is no more restful sense of unity than a sight of it catching the light from a westering sun throughout the summer and autumn. More prosaically, it is very easy to maintain, and was cheap to grow because it is the only rose I know that seeds freely. Apart from buying in three more to give me a start, I have been able to collect self-sown seedlings

ROSA RUBRIFOLIA (R. GLAUCA) Beautiful blue-grey foliage with red stems is the most distinctive feature of this species rose. Single flowers of a complementary tone of pink are carried along arching sprays. It seeds itself here and there (unusual in a rose) and has lovely red hips in early autumn.

from all over the garden to complete the line. It is of course quite right that this lovely rose should now be called *Rosa glauca* and not *Rosa rubrifolia* which is a misleading name, but I doubt if I shall be able to think of them as anything other than *rubrifolia*.

The tallest wall in the garden, southfacing, is at the opposite end of the orchard from the Ruins. Once the back wall of a tractor shed, it is now freestanding and nine feet high with a crumbly surface that needs pointing. Between the foot of the wall and the pigsties there used to be two hen coops and a rickety chicken-run. They looked easy enough to clear away so we decided to deal with them ourselves. One windy Saturday morning, feeling energetic, we dragged away the broken frames, the chicken wire and various feeding troughs and timbers. In an hour the ground was cleared and we examined it. Stone, we expected, as usual, but here the stone was organised. Prodding and scratching at it revealed that the chicken-run had been erected on the hidden floor of a medieval building.

To expose it was irresistible and we scraped and hosed and scrubbed until the whole extent was uncovered. Most of the stones were intact, with wide dividing lines marking walls and drains and door posts. It was only the floor of a stable, but it was our own archaeological find. Not exactly a dig, but to expose it was very hard work, cleaning it stone by stone, and it was late on Sunday night when the job was finished.

It runs the length of the wall – about twenty yards – and is ten feet wide with a very clear cobbled edge. Being continuous with the orchard-to-be, it became the orchard terrace-to-be. The floor is not made of the flagstones one might expect in a house. Flat paving stones would be slippery for hooves in a stable, and hard to drain. The stable stones are set on end, often eight or ten inches deep with a long narrow upper surface, packed tightly in rows but not cemented. When they are clean and seen across grass there is nothing nicer, unless perhaps the hooves of the big horses could be heard on them again, shifting and ringing in the stables.

For a year the terrace did remain clear, probably because the pressure of hosing had driven the accumulated earth from between each stone. But after a while the cracks filled up from nowhere and weeds began to put in an appearance, mostly in the broken and disturbed patches.

I started to think about planting. The idea of planting in stone was completely new to me, and the choice of plants was fairly simple. Being a level place and not a rockery, one cannot take it for granted that all alpines would necessarily be happy there, but spreading humps and clumps do well. The easiest and most obvious choice was thyme, and I found that thyme takes to stone much as a duck takes to water. A scrappy little root of *Thymus serpyllum* (the common creeping thyme) would make a mat three feet across in two years, springy and scented, flowering and even repeat-flowering each summer. Slightly less flat, the six-inch thymes, including the lemon-scented *T. citriodorus*, also cover the ground well. I also have one or two less vigorous but beautiful varieties, variegated in dark green and silver or gold. I have one particular thyme that is green and gold but I doubt if I could buy another, because the variety is called 'Green 'n' Gold', an irritatingly vulgar expression like 'Fish 'n' chips, frying t'nite'. Having to ask for it in a garden centre would bring out the 'that's what's wrong with the world today' in me.

Silver thyme grows on a single woody stem instead of spreading. It makes a neat and symmetrical clump which stands about eight inches high and can grow up to twelve inches across. I have used it round the septic tank with lavender behind it, and it makes the prettiest and smallest of hedges. The top of the septic tank itself is hidden by a *Chamaecyparis lateralis*. Ignorance about septic tanks is never bliss and just once there was a dreadful crisis. Every nose that passed that way twitched in amazement at the mingled scents of thyme and lavender and drains.

When any of the thymes gets too big on the orchard terrace I pull out the oldest and weediest parts and leave the new shoots creeping off in a different direction. From one year to the next the general shape shifts and spreads across the stone.

Low growing cistuses and their cousins the helianthemums, or rock roses, are planted in other patches where I can dig out a few inches of earth. I expect their roots are cool and moist under the floor and the stone is warm for them in summer. There are quite a lot of different cistuses, mostly pink or white, and some with a central purple blotch. They are all a bit tender, but cuttings from them root easily in a cold frame, so that losses can be replaced. I think of them as inhabitants of Greek hillsides, opening new flowers each morning and shedding them each evening.

There are three patches on the terrace where the stone is broken enough to take a bigger plant. One is at the far end, and a large rosemary spreads over it. Since there is nothing else nearby, it can sprawl in its happy inconsiderate way. Rosemary can be annoying when it refuses to be organised or tidy, but fortunately there is an upright form called 'Jessop's

Upright'. It is much more civilised among other plants but I like to have my negligent *Rosmarinus officinalis* too.

I put roses in the other two gaps in the terrace. They are there simply because at that time no other part of the garden was ready for me to take decisions about planting and I was impatient for my first old rose. I put in 'Gypsy Boy', one of my ideals in a Bourbon rose. I found that it is in fact not very old at all, being first grown at the beginning of this century. Its long strong sprays are massed with small, perfectly shaped, dark-red flowers with a tiny golden eye. As they grow older the blooms fade to a softer purple before they fall. In maturity it is a magical rose with the flowers lying layer upon layer, resting on each other. Planting it gave me a simple sense of achievement and delight and I sat back on my heels, willing it to thrive. Happily there was nothing to conflict with my placing of it. New tufts of thyme were starting nearby and across the grass the fruit trees were beginning to get on with their own lives.

There remained one gap in the terrace. I wanted another rose to be a companion to 'Gypsy Boy' but not to challenge it, and I chose 'York and Lancaster'. It was a name I had known for a long time and I thought the mixture of red and white would complement my lustrous 'Gypsy Boy'. It is a variegated Damask, and a much older rose, but I expected something more robust. It is not at all a case of, 'Now falls the crimson petal, now the white.' The flowers are a mixture of pale pink and paler pink, rather loose among light green leaves. There is in fact precious little York about it, and practically no Lancaster. At first I thought it was disappointing and anaemic, but I have come to be very fond of it now and it is, as I hoped, a good foil to 'Gypsy Boy'.

Apart from a few clumps of the black-leaved *Viola labradorica* and a funny prostrate rubus called *fockeanus* that wanders between the stones with little tough crinkly leaves, there is no room for more planting on the orchard terrace without cluttering it. Except of course for the little heartsease that sprinkle themselves about every year.

It sounds a straightforward place to manage, but a weeding problem built itself up over the years and has remained a perennial puzzle. However closely the stones are set, with no trace of earth between them, weeds find a way in. The insignificant greenish fuzz of early spring is deceptively unthreatening, but next time you turn round the whole terrace is blurred with short dense weeds. The sight of them generates a sense of depression, almost of dereliction, and the clarity of the place is gone. Handweeding is impossible – in two hours or so I can weed about two square yards but my fingers are by then too raw to do any more for about a week. Meanwhile half the weeds have probably broken off against the stones anyway, and will be back all too soon.

They will treat a paraquat weedkiller as only a temporary setback, with frail little reinforcements shoving up cheerfully. The terrace will be covered again in a trice if the ground itself is not put out of action for a whole season. The only thing is a systemic simazine weedkiller applied with desperate care and leaving a circle for handweeding round every patch of planting. Even a preparation that is advertised as non-spreading cannot be expected to resist rain. The first shower will wash it towards the plants and one can only watch helplessly.

Having reconciled myself to using simazine I found

that a hurdle still remained: if weedkiller goes straight
on to the weeds they die soon enough but lie about
looking like dead weeds which make the terrace even
gloomier than live weeds. So I have to do a sort of
phoney handweeding to pull off at least the tops of
the weeds. Even this is a time-consuming,
finger-scuffing job, and it is much more easily done
when the weeds are still tiny in early spring. This in
turn means that I am less likely to get consecutive fine
days when the weedkiller won't leak. And however
careful I am with the beastly stuff there are sure to be
many scorched and slaughtered little heartsease
because they are so scattered. This all sounds very
laborious, and indeed it is so, but in a fortunate year,
when the right things have flourished and the wrong
ones have perished, the sight of 'Gypsy Boy' falling on
to bare stones and scented thyme is worth it all.

Because of the tall beeches between the church and
the Ruins there is no more space for tree planting at
the end of the orchard. It is a large damp corner in
the deep shade cast by the high east window of the
church. It was evidently of no use to the farm and
when I first explored it I found a stronghold of ivy
and nettles growing on piles of indiscriminate
rubbish. Being the only place where there is leaf
mould, it was worth clearing, but for what? A
flowerbed would have been out of place and there
was not enough sunshine for most of the flowering
shrubs. I was not anxious to make more work, when
planting up the garden itself was so absorbing. At the
same time I did not want the back of the orchard to
tail off vaguely into a rubbish tip.

I took a chance on a few shrubs which have since
become established. One is a cornus of no particular
merit, another a winter-flowering *Viburnum*

fragrans, and the third a *Philadelphus coronarius*, a good solid shrub which would doubtless do better in drier soil. Between this framework I needed ground cover, and I planted gradually and without an overall plan. I even put leftovers in there, rejects that I didn't want to throw on the compost heap. At the very back I planted Russian comfrey whose creamy tubular flowers are inconspicuous but interestingly shaped. They do well in shade, as does the *Pulmonaria angustifolia* 'Munstead Blue' that I placed nearby. A cast-off from the garden is the pink *Geranium endressii*, obliging rather than exciting, which doesn't mind where it is asked to grow. Nearer the light, because I rated them as slightly more interesting, a couple of roots of *G. macrorrhizum* went in. Four different hostas, a couple of *Helleborus corsicus*, and an unnamed hypericum cutting (a Christmas present) just about filled the space. It seemed a bit colourless so I managed to find room for several small roots of polyanthus. None of it added up to very much and I paid little more attention to it. It was just the orchard end, a point at which one turns back when going round the garden.

All by itself, surreptitiously, it has changed. The ground cover really has covered the ground. The hostas and the hellebores give form. The geraniums give colour; there is always a scattering of pink flowers on *G. endressii*; *G. macrorrhizum* which has charming flowers has even more charming pink and green mottled foliage. In spring the polyanthus are as cheerful as clowns. But the delight of the place for me is that it has proved itself more or less independently. With very little tending or care from me the plants there have achieved a harmony and a communal character which I never expected.

It is the only part of the garden where the planting has a sense of continuous flow and one shape merges

HELLEBORUS CORSICUS
The thick hard leaves, each with three deeply-cut lobes and a toothed edge, make a strong architectural shape the year round. The pale buds remain tightly closed until March when their leaves lengthen. Then they stand above the leaves, clusters of nodding bells of a luminous green pallor.

naturally into the next. To an outside eye this is
possibly quite unremarkable. But in my flowerbeds
and borders I have constantly sought to define plants,
to give them their whole shape and value and I have
been afraid to blur outlines with too much
intermingling. Where I have used plants whose
natural habit is to spread, like catmints or geranium, I
have watched their roaming inclinations with
suspicion, and have even curtailed them. My casual
planting at the end of the orchard has brought more
success than I have deserved, and the plants
themselves must take the credit.

The question of definition often seems to arise in my
garden. In the orchard it was the question of the
terrace meeting with the orchard lawn. For the sake
of tidiness and also to simplify mowing, I made a very
narrow bed all along the edge dividing the two, and
planted a border of wild strawberries. They are tough
and easy to grow and if after two or three years they
get a bit straggly they can be tidied up and divided
without any trouble. Also, because they seed here and
there in the garden, there are always young plants to
hand, and they can be brought in to grow in gaps or
left to fill unconsidered corners, or just scrapped.
Wild strawberries have a small claim, too, to being the
link between the terrace and the orchard, being
alpines on the one hand, and fruit on the other. Their
fruit ripens in August and September, surprisingly
late. After trying a few woody and tasteless little
berries early in the season, it is a treat to find,
normally after a week in late summer with both rain
and sun, that they have ripened at last and that one
can fill a little bowl with juicy, scarlet, wild
strawberries with that special flavour that would cost
a fortune in a Paris restaurant.

As I fill my bowl the blackbirds and the wasps chew greedily at the apples and pears only a few yards away, but for some fortunate reason, which is a mystery to me, they have never touched the wild strawberries. It is hard to believe that a blackbird would not extend its normal beat by a few yards for the sake of such a luscious meal. However, I do notice more and more the extreme exactness of territory, particularly among small garden birds. The orchard and its terrace are mostly inhabited by insect- or seed-eaters. There is one pair of pied wagtails that flick and strut about the lawn, three or four assorted fly-catchers and warblers, and last year a family of linnets. The linnets nested in a honeysuckle, only five feet from the ground and not specially hidden. They sat on top of the wall and sang wonderfully for a month or two before taking flight. I hope they will come back.

The backdrop to the orchard is the Ruins and the church. These are flanked with great beech trees and black poplars and tall churchyard yews so there is in them a sense of bird life which is constantly active and busy. Apart from the neat little wagtails which are never still for a moment, and the small fry of tits and finches, there are nuthatches which dart in from the poplars in winter, looking for food, and a green woodpecker, often heard drilling, is occasionally to be seen when he drops in to inspect the lawn for ants. But most dominant are the rooks. They make their homes in the tall trees but their territory is the sky. Calling to each other, wheeling and diving as they keep us under surveillance, they form and reform, responding to every inflection of the wind and the weather. On a stormy evening it is not hard to see in them the Genius of the Place.

4

Trees and Shrubs

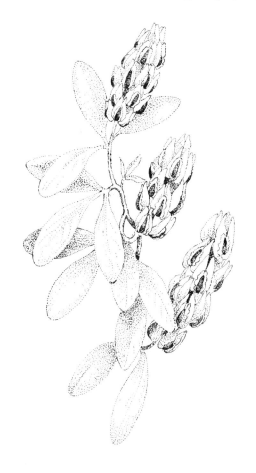

S hrubs are a significant part of garden life and their influence varies so much from one season to another that their planting needs care, and their habits can take one by surprise. One of the first shrubs I ever bought was a small nondescript thing with variegated leaves. It was to give a centre to an urn with geraniums and ivy, and it made quite a pleasant effect. Winter came, and the geraniums went. I looked more carefully at the variegated thing. It looked healthy enough, but slightly too large for its urn. Pat looked at it too, and said, 'That's a privet. It needs space.' A *privet*. How *boring*. There is a large corner between the field and the barn which was empty at that time. I had planned to plant a few shrubs there because it was out of reach of the mower. I put the privet in at the very back and left it alone and demoted. My shrubs would be

DIGITALIS AT THE END OF THE TITHE BARN
Foxgloves decided to thrust their way through every possible space between this planting of shrubs beside the tithe barn. They crop up in different places every year and can always be sure of a welcome in my garden.

63

definitely better class than mere privet, and if it could not survive behind them that would be just too bad. The classy shrubs took their time at first, but the privet thrived in its new space. Now there are two weigelas, one dark red and one cream; a kolkwitzia and a *Deutzia elegantissima*, all flowering beautifully and in great sprays. In the foreground, without claim to a well thought-out design, is a grey senecio plus a couple of low potentillas, with a scatter of self-sown foxgloves between them all and an *Arbutus unedo* at one end. But at the back, tall and in the form of a wide protective fan uniting them all, is my once-despised golden variegated privet, shining and evergreen.

To plant shrubs in their own place, which I suppose must be called a shrubbery, is comparatively easy. They need little more than shaping, and simple ground cover helps to keep down the weeds between them. It is the single-flowering shrubs growing in relation to herbaceous planting that can cause problems if they like to grow large and spread generously. Fully grown philadelphus such as the old-fashioned 'Belle Étoile' or double 'Virginal', pure white and strongly-scented, are great shrubs when they are in bloom, and deserving of space, but in the late summer their foliage is coarse and heavy, so they are usually best standing alone. I was surprised to find myself ruthless enough recently to take out a big old *Philadelphus* 'Belle Étoile' because it had become overbearing at the back of the herbaceous border. Its suckering shoots had spread out widely, and it was producing too few flowers in proportion to its size. I found it had taken over a great deal of ground which, after cleaning and feeding, could sustain a number of smaller plants including a beautiful small-scale philadelphus called 'Manteau d'Hermine'.

Many of the smaller shrubs are of great framework

value, and rarity is by no means a criterion. Senecio and southernwood, rosemary and the more tender cistuses, can all be placed in company or alone, to merge with one another or to stand out. Not all the smaller shrubs are grey, although many of the most useful tend to greyness. A few are more like tiny trees, such as the Russian almond which stands at the corner of my pump bed, or a prunus called *glandulosa* 'Albo-plena', a two-foot-high double white prunus far prettier than its name. My favourite hebe is also like a little candle-shaped tree, eighteen inches high. Its name is *Hebe hulkeana*, and since it is not very hardy I keep it in an urn. It has neat evergreen leaves and every June it is covered in tiny lilac-coloured flowers with a narrow white edge and a pink eye.

Trees are, if anything, even more important in the design and structure of a garden. One of the great fascinations of planting free-standing specimen trees is the question of how to use space. One can think first of the available space, and then visualise a tree within it. What height? What width? What habit, colour and texture? What soil? If these questions are all to be answered there are very few trees that will fit the bill in every respect, so the choice is simplified. Then the space fits itself around the tree and its identity becomes the place where that tree grows. This may be a successful result reflecting care and thought and making a satisfying entity. Or it may be that the significance of both the tree and the space is lost. That is, the tree was not chosen for its own character but was just a collection of suitable leaves and branches. And the space? Well, the space has been filled.

My own method of tree planting is much more risky, and has been known to end in tears if my choice proves to have been too amateur and self-indulgent. I buy a tree that I long to have and then look for the space. At first I could be lavish because the spaces were there. Enough for a copper beech near the road, a silky split-leaf beech near the Ruins, an oak tree by the field gate, a catalpa beyond the tithe barn, a silver birch behind the rose circle with a group of five different hollies close by. And for all the disasters of the wild garden the trees there are flourishing – the willows and the wild cherries, the chestnuts and two whitebeams.

But unless you have the dimensions of a park at your disposal, fingers become more acquisitive than green when it comes to trees, and sooner or later the planting has to stop. I have come to believe now that a really clear stretch of ground is a very dangerous place to grow a tree. It is undoubtedly a temptation if one can visualise a big free-standing tree in a certain place. But your clear stretch is immediately bisected, because even a small sapling stops the eye and a sense of distance and perspective has been sacrificed. Perhaps the trick is to see space as positive rather than negative, and to consider any prospective planting site from every possible angle.

One must also get the scale and proportion right. For example, I wanted a small tree – almost a miniature – to stand at the corner of the study garden. I planted an extremely small acer – A. *palmatum* 'Osakazuki', one of the Japanese maples turning beautifully through light green to pink and then to scarlet before its leaves fall. It may be that it would much prefer to be in stone less limy and stony, and that I have stunted it. If so, my unkindness has paid off, because it is exactly the right size for the proportions of Thyme Square, and shows no sign of growing any more.

In the same year that I planted the acer, at the opposite end of the scale and the opposite end of the garden, beside the tennis court, I planted a *Metasequoia glyptostroboides*. It is not often that one can plant potentially a very tall tree, and there is something exciting, even moving, about doing so. The metasequoia is not too difficult to find a home for because it is comparatively narrow so it will never shade a very large area. Nor will it cast broad leaves because although deciduous it is a conifer, and its needles take on gentle autumn colours before they fall. Its branches, which stick out at right angles when it is very young, in time curve sharply upwards quite close to the trunk, making a lovely vase shape. Mine is still young but after five almost stationary years it has begun to grow fast and very straight. I can look up into it now, instead of having to look down on to it. By sitting at its foot, so as to see it against the sky, I can just begin to visualise it as a mature tree, although it will by no means reach its full growth in my lifetime. I very nearly planted the metasequoia midway between the barns, in the mistaken belief that it would be a focal point and an improvement. I now realise that it would have destroyed the relationship of the barns to one another and interrupted the whole perspective.

METASEQUOIA GLYPTOSTROBOIDES
Although it is a conifer, this is a deciduous tree, and the leaves change from the pale larch-like green of spring to strong autumn colours before they fall in November. My young specimen is growing fast but I hardly expect to see it reach the height of this mature tree!

As it is, there is still an unbroken stretch of grass for a hundred yards or more beside the long axis of the barns and the tennis court, which is the better defined just because the metasequoia stands emphatically at the far end.

On each side of the drive there are two little trees which command my respect and care for two very different reasons. They are called *Aesculus pavia*, a small variety of chestnut which grows to a neat upright pyramid. They flower in August, bearing candles which are more sparse and elegant than the horse-chestnut. My two were given to me as cuttings by a friend who was a fine and original gardener. She was much-travelled and came to know some of the great gardens of the world and their owners. My *A. pavia* have an impeccable pedigree; they originated in the famous gardens of the Vicomte de Noailles, and my friend's cuttings are now fine trees from which my own cuttings were taken. They are now five years old and only eighteen inches high, which is my second reason for cosseting them. Most *Aesculus pavia* would be five feet high by the time they were five years old, but mine have twice been chewed and almost trodden into the ground by cows that strayed down the drive. So they are noble little survivors; one of them even flowered last summer. There is still one potential problem but I have closed my eyes to that. It is that their forbear in my friend's garden has reached a height of eighteen feet and is still growing. Two twenty-foot *Aesculus pavia* bordering the drive could be an embarrassment. I must build a bridge so that I can cross it when I come to it.

Another pair of trees that we planted are evergreens with a more particular purpose. I have never bothered with evergreens very much and have tended to be unsympathetic towards them because they don't *do* anything. But Peter has a great feeling for their dark outlines and strong shapes and I am beginning to appreciate them. The two that we planted several years ago, a cypress and a juniper, are intended to support three evergreen 'classics' in the churchyard, a cypress and two yews, which are immediately across our wall. They stand in superb relation to the south-east corner of the church and although they are still good for many years, they are old now. One day the two that we planted within a few yards of them will be very tall and will ensure that there is no sudden gap when the old ones go. The old ones, meanwhile, standing protectively behind our little orchard, provide unlimited safe housing for small birds. Every kind of tit and finch and wren and warbler flit between them, hidden in the dark branches as soon as they alight.

Our own juniper, now eight feet high, recently passed a milestone in its young life, a sort of tree puberty, when a blackbird took it seriously enough to nest in it and hatched her family successfully. The cypress, although taller, has no nest yet but I have made my own gesture of confidence towards it, by planting a *Tropaeolum speciosum* at its foot. This is related to the common nasturtium, with small scarlet flowers and bright green leaves. It loves to climb high into an evergreen; for instance in a tall yew-hedge where it can root well in the dark, in moist peaty soil. In late summer the brilliant little flowers string themselves like scattered jewels and necklaces across their dark background.

I always wanted to try to grow this but could find

no suitable site to offer it. I forgot all about it until I realised that the cypress would be tall enough to support one. Fortunately I came across a pot of it at someone's garden sale, well rooted and ready to go. Every winter it dies to the ground and emerges very late in the following spring. Once established it is quite hardy but I am relieved when mine does reappear because it seems so exotic and fragile. Perhaps the name *Tropaeolum speciosum* suggests a special tropical tenderness, and of course the ordinary nasturtium, although very tough and workaday, is an annual.

By the path leading from the field gate to the tithe barn and the granary is a very large mulberry bush. It barely survived its first summer which was the drought of 1976. Watering was banned, so I fed it with bowls of washing-up water seasoned with grease and Fairy Liquid which apparently suited it. I intended it to be a mulberry tree, but it decided to grow into a huge round bush, obscuring our breakfast view of the fields and, more recently, of the pools. Sitting over a cup of coffee on the terrace, my affection for it diminishes, but then I think a mulberry bush is a fine thing to have, and who could cut one down? I can look at the view from somewhere else.

Also, between the granary and the tithe barn is an acer similar to one that I saw growing, cramped, in a London garden. I thought it would look beautiful in the country so I tracked one down and planted it three years ago. It is called *Acer saccharinum* 'Laciniatum Weirii' and will I hope be smaller than the big *Acer saccharinum*. It is very sweepy and well-shaped, with deeply cut leaves which are silvery

TROPAEOLUM SPECIOSUM
A perennial climber that starts out of the ground in May, and scrambles up into, preferably, a dark evergreen. Both the emerald leaves and the scarlet flowers are brilliant and delicate, springing from the narrowest of wiry stems. Its roots like to be well-shaded, and the whole plant dies down to nothing in the late autumn.

on the reverse. It has plenty of space to grow
free-standing and elegant; a permanent shape which I
expect to be increasingly satisfying as it matures and
develops.

Trees – and especially trees in Irish hillside gardens –
have a special fascination for me. A couple of years
ago I saw the gardens of Muckross Abbey in County
Cork for the first time, and fell in love with them. It
was a windy October day, and as I stood under the
great oak trees, a romantic and foolhardy vision came
to my mind of my great-grandchildren playing in the
shade of oaks from Muckross. All around me, the
green Irish sward beneath the huge oak trees was
covered with acorns. I took a handful home in my
pocket and put them between damp tissues in a
plastic bag. On the way back to England I forgot about
them. When I found them three weeks later, the
tissues were a tangled mass of hopeful roots and
sprouts. But little roots that have started in moisture
find it hard to survive the transition to soil, and my
acorns did not, alas, transplant.

I persuade myself that it was just as well and that
the oaks would have been a liability. But – let me
confess it – I am only partly convinced.

5

The Coming of the Herb Garden

O n the right-hand side of the drive was a paddock. It must have been unused for many years when we arrived and was inhabited by our old friends the nettles and thistles. At its southern end, the back wall of the woodshed and another wall separated it from the rest of the land, so there was no need to see it as any part of an overall plan for the garden. With a bit of fencing it would have made a very good home for a donkey.

Or rather two donkeys, because one would get lonely. I was tempted for a while with such a rural notion, and fancied myself arriving home from London, and going out to the paddock with carrots in my pockets. I would lean over the gate and the donkeys would come trotting gratefully and meekly to stand near me. But I soon had to admit that I had not the slightest need of one donkey, let alone two, and would very soon get bored with them. Anyway, they would not like to be left in a thistly paddock while I went to London for days at a time. I remembered one old family joke, 'We had a donkey once. No sooner had we taught it to go without food and water than the stupid thing died.' So no donkey.

This meant that I could not designate the weedy strip as a 'paddock', and had to do something about it – as an approach to the garden it was discouraging. I sprayed and dug and rotavated for a couple of years, ignoring it in-between-times. It was work in progress so at least there was promise in it. Eventually a moderately clean piece of ground resulted, and I found myself wondering what to do with it.

Being separate from the emerging garden, and of a reasonable size (fifty yards by fifteen yards) it naturally became the vegetable garden. It was a relief to indulge a feeling of control over one corner of the place without any sense of long-term commitment.

The first spring, with broad beans unfurling, young carrots feathery and onions spiky, all obedient, neat and fastcropping, gave me a wonderfully sunny sense of achievement. Mange-tout peas grew easily, the French-beans were abundant, and perpetual spinach was a joy. Leeks were no problem and runner-beans made me feel I had arrived. I only once tried a few cauliflowers, and never did graduate to brassicas, which sounded too professional for me. But I did sow five sorts of lettuce and was so delighted when they began to grow that I could hardly bring myself to thin them out to their proper spacing.

What I had not bargained for was the intensity of the labour, and the tyranny of the timing. The weeding and the watering, the thinning and the staking were endlessly demanding. I learned that vegetable gardening is no fun if you do it against the clock. My romantic vision was of strolling out and picking a basket of peas ('Bring me the full of the dish', my mother would say in Ireland) and then sitting on the kitchen step in the evening sun, shelling them into the saucepan with a handful of mint thrown in. It does happen, and is a lovely exercise. Even tugging leeks out of iron-hard ground with frozen fingers can have its own pleasure (though this is best enjoyed in retrospect) and the joy of eating one's own freshly-picked vegetables never fails. But the effort was too costly for me in the long run, simply because there was too much else to do.

As they ripened, I discovered that the high price of greengrocers' mange-tout peas must be a reflection of the tiresomeness of picking them; and that the tenderness of beans is altogether in the moment. There never seemed to be anyone around to eat them

at the exact moment when we should be indulging in
an orgy of baby broad-beans.

The corollary was hours spend in preparing and
blanching and packing for the deep freeze, and that
very soon palled.

I have nothing against growing vegetables and my
grumbling is only because I could not spare the time
to do it properly. So I struggled on for four years,
contracting the vegetable garden into a slightly
smaller area each year. The mice, the blackbirds and
the caterpillars had their share, but I was
philosophical about that. However, one early July day
I drove down from London and turned in at the gate
to see a dismal sight. My vegetable garden, at the
height of its season, had been stripped bare and the
unripe crops had been trampled or ripped up. They
were only passing vandals, and probably would never
have returned, but they tipped the scales for me.

That autumn, gradually digging up my erstwhile
vegetable garden, I wondered again how to use a
large rectangle of spare ground. The family thought of
a croquet lawn and it seemed a natural place for it. So
a croquet lawn it became. We hired a JCB which
levelled it in a day and left low sloping banks along
three sides. It is a bit long and thin for a serious
croquet lawn, but the hoops make it convincing
enough.

Along the three banked sides I planted twenty-six
'Nevada' roses. They are maturing now, and their
central stems look quite gnarled like old tree roots. In
early June, their great sprays are massed with flat
creamy blossoms, arching to seven feet or more. In
spite of the great generosity of their bloom, the single

wide flowers lie so peacefully along their branches that you could never think of a 'Nevada' rose as voluptuous or luscious. It is the largest shrub rose I know, and quite recent. If I had bred it, I would have considered my life well spent.

The fourth side of the croquet lawn is edged by the drive and along its border I planted four 'Constance Spry' modern shrub roses, with four 'Président de Sèze' on one side of them and four 'Bonn' on the other. As opposed to 'Nevada' nothing could be more voluptuous than the huge 'Constance Spry' with its lovely double pink blooms rolling and tumbling over their wooden stakes. They need a lot of spraying and tidying, and although they are wonderful in their blowsy way, there is a month or more after the flowering when the plants are rather leggy and bare and the black spot shows through. Even worse in that respect are the 'Bonn' which is another modern shrub rose. They are 'cheap and cheerful' and very obliging about recurrent sprays for picking. But as soon as their first flowering is over, mine become almost completely defoliated for a while, which, as they are about six feet high, is rather depressing. This year I shall treat them almost as Hybrid-tea roses and cut them back hard and very short.

The 'Président de Sèze', at the far end of the drive beyond the 'Constance Spry', are altogether a different matter. They are characteristically tough *gallica* roses, with healthy suckering stems that grow densely to about four feet. In late June they are covered in beautifully quartered pink roses which open from dark pink buds and then brim into purple as the outer petals open fully. If the 'Bonn' roses do not survive my tough pruning I shall replace them with 'Président de Sèze'.

This line of roses, 'Bonn', 'Constance Spry' and the

'Président de Sèze', are the result of completely ignorant planting on my part. They don't relate to each other in any way. No one could possibly look at them and say, 'What a good idea to put those next to each other.' Fortunately they are mostly seen in passing as people drive in or out, and they make a very jolly show. I pick a lot, too.

The 'Nevada', on the other hand, are well placed, just far enough apart to display their whole shape. They are the easiest possible roses to manage and hardly need touching. I occasionally cut out an old shoot from the base or shorten a few of the longest sprays to keep them out of the way of the mower. Of course the 'Nevada', starting to flower in early June, are over well before the others start, which is a good thing, because I like them to have their moment – and it is quite a short moment – without competition or distraction. By the time the pinks and reds along the drive come into flower, the 'Nevada' are just letting us have a continuing sprinkle of blooms to remind us of their earlier glory.

All these roses bordering the croquet lawn, about forty in all, have one monster feed of horse manure during the winter. This seems to keep most of them healthy, and the great consolation after the end of the season is the sight, by September, of strong new shoots pushing up through the centres of the shrubs, promising next year's flower-power.

Nevertheless, these things did not (except for the croquet hoops) establish themselves overnight, and meanwhile I was mourning the loss of my vegetable plot. I decided to console myself with herbs. Instead of a few clumps of chives and parsley outside the kitchen window, I laid out a proper little classic herb garden, standing alone and picked out in flagstones. It adjoins one end of the croquet lawn, separated from it only by a line of the 'Nevada' roses. The small symmetrical beds with their rectangular stone edge are divided up by paving just wide enough to walk on, and in the centre is a plain stone sundial with a beautiful face.

It is a simple theory, and simple in execution too. Very tall herbs grow at one end, very short ones nearest the centre, middle-sized and unusual ones along the sides, and shrubby ones at the other end. By 'very tall', I mean that two angelicas grow right at the back, and their huge greenish flower-heads reach to a statuesque six feet. A plant may last two or three years, but if it dies during the winter there are always thousands of seedlings to be weeded out anyway, so replacements are invariably to hand in early spring. Alongside the angelicas are dill and the bronze and green fennels, elegantly feathery and also easily replaceable when necessary. Their seedlings are less abundant but always reliable. In the same bed, in front of these, are a camphor on one side, and tarragons and sweet cicely on the other. Camphor makes a perennial clump with unwieldy rigid roots which are hard to lift or divide. Every year or so, when it gets too big, I just have to hack a few bits off. The sweet cicely is like a soft delicate fern, very pretty early in the year but easily bedraggled later. Its generic name is *Myrrhis odorata*.

Round the base of the sundial and in the small beds nearest to it are the low-growing herbs. Symmetrical clumps of chives come back first after the winter, their strong grassy tips showing encouragingly even through snow. Parsley, next to the chives, tends to get out of step and grow either too strongly or too

ANGELICA
Striking umbelliferous flowers of a greenish-yellow colour stand above tall stems and deeply cut leaves. They sow seed all around, growing tall and dying away with equal casual abandon.

weakly. Some of the plants rush into thick flowering stems (which need to be taken off at once) and others continue green and curly through the winter for a second season. I put in a few seeds each spring to fill any gaps, and before sowing them I leave them in the fridge for a week or two. This kids them into believing that spring has arrived when they are taken out, so they germinate more quickly in the ground.

Sweet woodruff, a small mint called pennyroyal, and a little collection of thymes, including the lemon scented *Thymus citriodorus*, are also arranged near the sundial. Sweet woodruff spreads a neat and hardy perennial mat throughout the summer, only a few inches high, and its white starry flowers appear in June, covering the whole plant. A few sprigs of it left overnight in a jug of cold white wine makes a delicious summer drink before Sunday lunch. I saw a dyer's woodruff in the Chelsea Physic Garden, even prettier and several inches taller, but I have never been able to get hold of a plant. Pennyroyal, which is also a mat, but of compact dark green leaves, seems to me to have no particular interest or virtue apart from its intriguing name. Except that it is an abortifacient which may or may not be a virtue. To the left and right are two square beds, one crammed with five sorts of mint and the other with two sorts of marjoram, the ordinary one having unfortunately nearly succeeded in crowding out the golden one.

Opposite them are the odds and ends, where symmetry takes second place. There are the winter and summer savories, tough little shrubby plants with bright blue and mauve flowers rather like heather. Salad burnet and chervil together are light and lacy, and I would place coriander in the same category. They all have a spicy fragrance in salads.

Much more interesting among the odds and ends

SWEET WOODRUFF
A neat little herb with tiny starry flowers in late May and June. The leaves are shaped like ruffs but the 'wood' in the name may be misleading. Mine thrives in full sun in the herb garden, and has grown into a mat that completely fills the square of space allotted to it.

are the plants with intriguing names that sometimes appear in small pots on the trestle tables marked 'Herbs' outside garden centres. I have found three so labelled recently, and all of them have developed unexpectedly. Vervain is of course not rare – it is the French name for *Verbena officinalis*, a wiry, attractive plant about two feet high, its flowers like purple fingertips on skinny arms. Another was wall germander, – an extremely small cutting, scarcely rooted. After some searching, the books told me this was *Teucrium chamaedrys* which likes the shelter of a wall. It is now quite a decent little plant, a foot high with pink flowers, and leaves like a miniature ceanothus. However, it does not give a very herbal impression.

My third mystery-pot turned out to be a jackpot. I picked it up three years ago, a miserable little thing called motherwort. I had never heard of it before nor have I since, and have so far only found one reference to it which gives its Latin name as *Leonurus cardiaca*. It is certainly the most outstanding plant in the herb garden. It has dark-green pointed hairy leaves, growing on strikingly upright sturdy stems to a true goblet shape, three feet high. Small mauve flowers appear in little whorls all the way up and down each stem in the axils of the leaves. Its stems are hollow, so I feared the crown might rot in winter, but once established it is a fully hardy perennial. It also seeds freely, which pleases me because I enjoy giving my friends seedlings which grow into this fine, aristocratic and little-known plant.

The end bed is perennial and shrubby. An upright rosemary is placed in each corner, balanced by a southernwood (*Artemisia abrotanum*). A small bay occupies one side and a purple sage the other.

MOTHERWORT
Hardly ever described in gardening books or listed in catalogues, although it is easily grown and makes an impressive plant.

It is not a particularly original herb garden, but it is a
complete thing in itself, a funny little microcosm of
garden life which I find very satisfying. In the spring
and the late autumn when I weed it and sweep it, it is
definitively weeded and swept; I can feel the job is
done. What I really like about it is that in early spring
all is tidily organised in a neat pattern with everything
in its appointed place. The beds with the rosemary
and the cut-down southernwood are a bit bare so I
sow small rows of spring onions and radishes and
even a few compact lettuces like 'Tom Thumb'. These
accentuate a sense of order and control which is
extremely rare in the rest of my garden.

Then, very gradually at first, my little regiment is
invaded and the rabble moves in surreptitiously.
Borage seedlings appear first, then clary, the annual
salvia, and golden feverfew. Before long everything is
growing at a vast speed and the neat outlines are
blurred. Chives are the first to flower, then the borage
lolling over the paths. By July the whole army is
disaffected and all traces of discipline lost. The mints
scramble to two feet high or more, the ordinary
Mentha spicata mixing with the pale and
woolly-leaved applemint which grows cheek to cheek
with a beautiful dark form of peppermint which is
hardly less vigorous. Marjoram flowers spread across
their neighbours and even the choosy tarragon looks
unkempt and straggly. Wide yellow umbrellas of
fennel and dill form an airy background with a mass
of creamy anthemis daisies alongside and the round
heads of angelica towering over them all.

I let everything flower and seed until September
when the rioting dies down and the top-heavy fennel
is sprawling to one side. Then I feel disapproval of the
'party's over' impression and gradually begin cutting
back. When everything is weeded and swept once

more, and the herbs lie demurely within their stone boundaries, the sundial is again the quiet focus, and I can still pick the few herbs I need for the kitchen.

Throughout the summer I use any number of these herbs chopped up in salads. I am deliberately not too precise about which should predominate, so that flavours and textures vary from one day to the next – I have to admit that appreciation of my salads is variable too.

When September comes, or earlier if the herbs begin to decline, I chop up bunches of mint and chives and some of the annual herbs, and freeze them. Mixed with a little water in ice-trays they make cubes which I use through the winter. When they are thawed they are a bit too soggy to be used in salads, but they provide a good flavour in cooking, fresher than a dried bouquet garni.

The herb garden is not the only place where I grow herbs. Thyme is an integral part of another small area of the garden – a little terrace on a site which must have been intrinsic to farmyard life from the fifteenth century.

A medieval stable floor was revealed when the original woodshed, nearly adjoining the main part of the house, was converted into a study. As the builder's rubble was cleared away around the old door of the woodshed, we found stone laid exactly as it was in the nearby orchard terrace. It extends at present over a square about as big as the little study itself. There may be more that we have not exposed, and probably it runs under the existing house floor. We cleaned it and I put in a few roots of creeping thyme in the broken patches, which very quickly spread over large areas. They are mixed now with one or two saxifrages although rather too much moss has crept in. Occasionally I harden my heart and pull out whole strips where the thyme has been most heavily invaded with moss. The effect of an old stone terrace with patches of thyme on it is a great deal more satisfactory than a blanket of thyme with glimpses of stone showing through. Because it lies in front of the study it could be called the study terrace. It is, in fact, Thyme Square, and it is different in one respect from the whole of the rest of the garden: in Thyme Square there is more thyme than space, whereas everywhere else I find that I have a great deal more space than time.

I know that to some gardeners a herb garden is a prissy milk-and-water concept. To one author whose work I greatly admire the very thought is anathema. He wouldn't be seen dead in a herb garden and in one of his books he explains why in a heartfelt hymn of hate. The fact that I have not come across any warning signs of bias, sexism or prejudice anywhere else in his garden writing makes his diatribe the more startlingly impressive.

Nevertheless, I enjoy my herb garden. I find it amusing, wonderfully smelly, partly edible, robust and enormously varied. Not to mention romantic.

6

The Wild Garden,

or Sowing Dragon's Teeth

he only project in the garden that I approached with complete confidence was the wild garden. I believed that I had only to cherish a bit of spare land and allow a kind of super-meadow to spring up.

Admittedly Cotswold limestone is not Downland chalk, but even without indigenous harebells and lady's slipper, there are thousands of wildflower seeds to be sown. I think I expected that the very fact that I was so enlightened as to believe in a wild garden – the idea was just becoming fashionable – somehow entitled me to success. Not much to ask of Mother Nature? Too much it seems, because she has administered a reproof that has been more a kick in the teeth than a slap on the wrist every year since I started the whole disastrous scheme. I am now at square minus five.

The siting of it was simple, and a natural choice. We built a tennis court, an admitted and successful trap to entice our children to visit us at weekends, very soon after we arrived. The court is behind the barns, and between it and the field there remained a strip of ground, itself about the same size as the tennis court. On it were the remains of old henhouses, which could be torn up and removed without much difficulty. My first and most basic mistake was to deal with this casually instead of thoroughly. A certain amount of metal and concrete and wire remained in the ground; I ignored it. 'It's meant to be wild. It'll soon cover over,' I thought. There was so much else to do in those days. While my back was turned it did indeed cover, and with enormous speed. From the field, with which it is continuous, there spread a heavy crop of nettles and docks. Even a champion hand-weeder like myself must quail in front of a solid breast-high wall, the length and breadth of a tennis court, of docks and nettles in mid-summer.

'Never mind, we'll rotavate it and clean it before the autumn' was my next thought. The ignored concrete and metal proved more stubborn than any rotavator blade. 'Very well, we'll weedkill,' was my obvious response to that. I chose a weedkiller that was strong enough to do the job without poisoning the earth itself for any length of time, and sprayed the whole area, very expensively, with glyphosate. The impressive result was satisfactorily hideous and lasted until the spring, when I was far too busy with the rest of the garden to get near the tennis court, let alone to the far side of it. Naturally, one spraying had not been enough. Healthy young shoots of nettles and docks, backed up by plenty more invading from the field, were back in strength. The next attempt was on the same lines, but much more thorough and much more expensive. The result was only very slightly more effective.

Finally the ground seemed clear enough to sow grass seed. I had read that grass should be established before wildflower seeds were introduced. God knows what I sowed, but the grass came up like dragon's teeth. I thought I had chosen the right kinds, and the first green flush was wonderfully convincing. It flowered too, which was very pretty, with aesthetic textures and colours; waving tall grasses mingled in the early summer breezes. Every one of those grass seeds that fell to the ground must have germinated. By the following year the wild garden was a solid green mat. I scattered some wildflower seeds broadcast, in the forlorn hope that the very smallest of them might land in the tiniest chink between the grasses. No luck. The only growing thing that could penetrate this thicket came from underneath, and by

FRITILLARIA MELEAGRIS
The Snake's Head Lilies look their best in grass which is their natural meadow habitat. But their narrow leaves die down slowly while you wait impatiently to cut the grass. In most groupings there are a few white ones, a lovely variation on the mysterious mottled purples. The little knobbly bulbs are best planted on their sides so that the rain cannot penetrate their delicate crowns and make them liable to rot.

the end of the year the nettles were back in force, bonny and strong. I stood in the midst of them, and though I am not usually given to paranoia, I could have sworn that they were grinning at me.

One night of thunder and pounding rain laid the heavy-headed grasses to the ground so that they were inaccessible to the scythe. As soon as they began to lift we tried a rough mower cut combined with the scythe, but by that time the grasses had sown their seeds again. There had been noticeably fewer of the beautiful, nodding, grass flower-heads, the pink and silvery ones, and the feathery delicate ones. They had been shouldered out by that heavy tussocky stuff, the coarsest of the meadow grasses.

My attitude to the whole scheme was no longer patient or hopeful; by now, it was savage. Something had to be done so I cleaned some small patches of ground and sowed wildflower seeds into them. A few young trees also grew in the wild garden (I refuse to stop calling it that, or even to use inverted commas) and round them I put in small wild daffodils, a few *Fritillaria meleagris*, and at the far end, bluebells under the single cherry tree.

Along the boundary with the field, I had planted sixteen *Salix daphnoides*. The point of this was to have an informal hedge, about four feet high, of these purple-stemmed willows, bushy but not dense, and only slightly more sophisticated than their cousins, the crack willows, across the field. Eleven of them were dealt with by rabbits in the first week that snow fell, which was a couple of months after they were planted. The rabbits, short of food, debarked them, which is one of their nastier winter habits. Once it has been nibbled all the way round no young tree can survive. Never mind. You can cut a shoot of a willow and just stick it in the ground. They *always* take. This

SALIX DAPHNOIDES
Most willows, including S. daphnoides, *are easy to cultivate. First-year shoots with lovely violet stems show to best advantage if the plant is hard pruned, almost to the ground, in February. Those that escaped my knife grew tall, and have rewarded me with their silver 'pussies'.*

in fact proved to be the case, and allowing for more rabbit damage and a lot of fiddling with wire to protect them, several shoots did strike and are growing. The edge of the field is of course the front line as far as nettles are concerned, so the willow shoots too occasionally fall victim to successive slaughtering efforts, but there is at least an impression of willows in a rough line. However, it is not in any sense a hedge.

For two years I left the original survivors without cutting them back to keep the shoots young and purple-stemmed. I expect I just forgot. In any case, I was battling away in the wild garden one morning and chanced to sit back on my heels and look up. It was very early April, and I saw for the first time silver pussy-willows against the brilliant blue sky. Three of the surviving trees had shot up much taller than I had realised, and I found myself, to my unexpected joy, possessor of my very own pussy-willows. Now I can cut long wands of them each year to bring into the house, but it is the sight of them standing so innocently against the clean skies of April that makes me catch my breath.

As to my wild garden, I suppose that apart from my failure to sow the right grass, my downfall has been due to bad timing. To have cut the grass at the right moments in the year, to have kept up with the weeds whenever they broke through, to have given the flower seeds their best chance to germinate, all these would have helped it to establish.

Probably I shall turn a blind eye to it all for a while, pushing my way through the rank jungle only to gaze at the pussy-willows on rare April days. It is surely the one piece of land in the Cotswolds with the very least number of wildflowers growing in it. Other than a few brave bulbs, I have been able this year to point to one magnificent teazle, two white campions, a battered foxglove and a stolen cowslip root. It was only stolen from a corner of my own field but even so I dug it up very surreptitiously.

One day I will start all over again. I will read the books, stick to the rules, and not cut any corners. When I have time.

The Lake District

Four ducks on a pond
And a blue sky beyond.
Such a little thing to remember for years
To remember with tears.

hat quatrain about the ducks has an infallibly sentimental effect on me and I feel a lump in my throat whenever I think of it. 'To remember with tears' is not explained. The tears are for a private idyll lost, I suppose, and lost innocence. The line conjures up infinitely more than the small statement itself. Probably because my mother used to quote it, and because of that First World War period, I envisage a grimy young Tommy in a reverie about Home as he sits in his trench before going Over the Top.

The wistfully romantic verse slipped in and out of my mind from the moment we began to consider bringing water into the garden. As soon as the idea became a physical reality and we had begun the process of digging out huge holes, the ducks and the blue sky beyond receded into the very far distance. Instead, the image of World War One dominated the scene. The site turned into a sea of mud and clay, with a few forlorn stakes leaning towards each other, marking nothing in particular. So it remained through a wet autumn, an icy winter, and a cold spring. If only a famous director had been looking for a film set to make a movie of the Battle of the Somme. We could have stuck a bayonet into the mud next to the stakes, with a tin helmet tilted over it and a roll of barbed wire alongside. The cameras could have moved in, churning up even more mud, and we would have made a fortune, enough to pay for the most elaborate of pools.

At first the notion of bringing water into the garden at all was completely foreign to me. A complex and expensive piece of garden engineering that seemed to me unnecessary and irrelevant. Peter, on the other hand, had always wanted it. He saw it clearly and with great enthusiasm and was convinced from the start that water would be a marvellous addition to the garden. He coaxed me along with talk about a duck-pond, to reassure me that water could be in keeping with my farmyard ethic, and I could only agree that four ducks on a pond would be very acceptable. He put less emphasis, at first, on his more complicated schemes and plots, and by the time I could begin to visualise his plans, I was converted.

There was only one part of the garden that could possibly be used for water, and once we recognised it everything fell into place. From the house one can look through a gap of fifty yards between the barns, over a seven-foot wall and thence across the fields. The wall was the back of a long milking shed. We took the black roof off it in the same way that we had taken the roof off the tractor shed, leaving the pillars and the beams in place. To the left rises the dovecot's high circular wall, and to the right is the square walled paddock behind the tithe barn. The cattle used to be driven in there from the field to wait their turn for milking. The whole place was logically for the use of cattle and there was no feeling of garden or potential garden about it.

There was, however, one peculiarity which was a change in the level of the ground. A retaining wall runs parallel to the erstwhile cowshed which was six feet lower than the ground between the barns. A wide gap at the dovecote end of the retaining wall leads down into the long narrow rectangle which used to contain the whole of the cowshed and its forecourt. Almost fully walled, this has a completely different atmosphere from any other part of the garden. Had it

been a garden in itself it would undoubtedly have
been a proper sunken garden. As it was, it was at least
sunk, and we began to think of planning a pool with
that in mind. My only opportunity for real symmetry
and formality was there, but not in the accepted
eighteenth-century sense. That would have been
impossible because of the confidently medieval
dovecot dominating one end, and the weight of the
oak pillars and beams along the old wall. It seemed
possible that mystery, rather than elegance, could set
the tone. The planting certainly would not allow of
even a hint of herbaceousness, so I began to search
the catalogues for sculptural shapes and ornamental
foliage.

There was a thick collar of nettles all along the
retaining wall, deepening at the corners and even
curling up out of the wall itself. Embarking on my
usual campaign to reclaim the ground from their grip,
I thought of the generations of cattle that had stood
patiently there. I promised myself that for once I
would strike it rich with well-manured workable soil.
To my great surprise and disappointment, the soil
over that whole sunken-garden-to-be was a mixture of
clay – like dark red toffee – and gravel.

Eventually, and with the greatest difficulty, I
succeeded in planting one long primary row of
Helleborus corsicus. All the plants were brothers. One
year the only Corsican hellebore I ever bought
decided to seed itself voluminously. It was two years
old when it suddenly surrounded itself with offspring.
I managed to collect them all (there were about fifty)
and after loosening the gravelly clay with peat and a
little extra soil, I planted them along the back of the
cowshed wall. The original hellebore is still in a
strategic corner of the herbaceous border, and
because he is Corsican, and the progenitor of so

many, I think of him as the Godfather. Nowadays, he produces only the occasional seedling, enough to fill a gap here and there. I wonder why he was so aptly bountiful that one year.

Now that they are fully grown and established, the hellebores set the style without being conspicuous. Their fine stiff leaves keep their shape and colour until well into summer. By the time I cut them away the new shoots are already strong in the centre of the plant, ready to spread open when they meet the light fully. As I clear up the old rattling spikes the air is full of their musky scent, like an animal in the forest.

Whether grown singly in a row or in a clump, *Helleborus corsicus* is a most valuable plant. The flower heads, pale green above the dark leaves, remain closed and waiting from early autumn. Eventually their stems lengthen and the brilliant pale green cups open in early spring, remaining erect and still for week after week.

HELLEBORUS CORSICUS
The thick hard leaves, each with three deeply-cut lobes and a toothed edge, make a strong architectural shape the year round. The pale buds remain tightly closed until March when their leaves lengthen. Then they stand above the leaves, clusters of nodding bells of a luminous green pallor.

94

Very little more headway was made with the planting
in that sunken place until we took, metaphorically,
the plunge into water. Then the retaining wall came
into its own. We had long deliberated between what
the books call a 'formal' and an 'informal' pool. The
two levels offered us the answer – two pools. The
upper one, between the barns and on flat grass, would
be informal, and down in the long rectangle would
be the formal one. The whole concept fitted neatly
in both scale and practicability, and there was a bonus.
We had worried about the likelihood of a still pool
becoming stagnant and dirty: with two pools close to
each other with a five foot difference in their levels, we
could surely devise a way for the water to circulate.

I still had one reservation. I could think of no

The relationship between the upper and lower pools.

possible rationalisation to convince me that a formal
ornamental pool would be in keeping with an old
cowshed. Concern to preserve the atmosphere of the
place had become my accustomed frame of mind.
Had our sunken area been near the centre of the
garden we would not even have considered
importing water into such an unnatural setting. But a
broken-down cowshed in poor ground is not
clamouring to be lovingly redeemed, or even to be
reunited with anything else.

It is, moreover, completely hidden until you reach

it, and together with its unexpectedly rectangular shape, these were ideal characteristics. It was our one possible space for formal water, and blessedly easy to connect with the upper pool which was to be a simple sheet of water on grass. I very soon came to terms with the double vision.

I bought books and was immediately discouraged. With dogged honesty the writers warned me of the pitfalls, the disappointments, even the dangers, of water gardens. The chapters of instructions, clear and foolproof as they were, depressed me even more. I knew for certain that I could never work according to the necessarily strict rules of depths and angles that the dedicated pond-maker loves. I foresaw months of inadequate and frustrating digging and measuring, and then realised that fortunately the job was far too big for us to attempt by hand anyway. Whatever the end result might be, a machine must come and dig the holes.

We consulted a man whose name is known over many counties by all who have to do with lakes or streams or blowing things up. He is Mr Jack Hatt, and nowadays I believe he does most of the work with water, and his sons concentrate more on the blowing up. With his tweeds and his boots and his dog, he arrived one day with his fund of knowledge and experience about what water will do or will not do, and why. Clambering stiffly out of his muddy Land Rover (I believe one leg was once involved rather too closely with the blowing-up side of the business) he walked over and over the ground, looking at it from different angles. Sometimes he shook his head; several times he prodded his stick through the turf and stood, considering. We watched him, expecting a verdict. But his mind was roaming the waterways of England and his advice to us was not to be so instantly

Looking out from the big door towards the summerhouse.

The Herb Garden with the sundial in the middle and the *rugosa* roses behind.

The upper pool is separated from the lower by an old retaining wall. They are connected by the waterfall and little pool in the left-hand corner.

Across the pump bed in high summer, looking towards the house. To the right of the big door are the rose, 'Caroline Testout', and a *Hydrangea petiolaris*.

The herbaceous border.

A view across the orchard terrace, past 'York and Lancaster', to the church. The rose in the foreground is 'Kathleen Harrop', against the Pearly Gate.

Rosa 'Nevada'. A young plant in bloom.

Rosa 'Gypsy Boy'.

Clematis 'Comtesse de Bouchaud' in an old apple tree on the lawn.

Rosa 'Rosa Mundi'.

The dovecot from across the lower pool. The roses are 'Leverkusen' and 'Highfield' on the sides of the Golden Gate and in the foreground the angelica is in flower.

The steps through the Golden Gate lead to the church and the Ruins in the distance. In the bottom left-hand corner, the edge of the lower pool can be seen with its border of *Alchemilla mollis*.

From the *rubrifolia* wall, one looks back across the orchard lawn towards the back of the house.

Rosa 'Charles Austin'.

distilled. 'Ah,' he would say, 'Lord So and So had ground very like this. Nasty stuff. His lake was causing trouble, and we had the devil's own job with it. In the end we had to . . .' and so on. We got so involved with his fascinating descriptions of Lord So and So's problems ('I expect you know the place. Ever fished it? You should. Excellent in the middle of the season'), that our own little pools would be forgotten. We would be shaking hands over a drink and then waving goodbye to the muddy Land Rover before we remembered the next crucial question we had been going to ask.

But Mr Jack Hatt knows what he is doing, and so long as he does not feel that you are going against nature, he is on your side. The big machines were organised in no time at all. It was the middle of September when they came, during a long spell of beautiful dry weather, and the ground was perfect. By the grace of God the huge earth-mover could just tiptoe down the drive and across the grass without crunching up any roses or young trees on its way. Mr Hatt had advised us against using a plastic liner, and we agreed, feeling instinctively that it was nasty artificial stuff. The areas concerned were in any case too large to be easily lined with plastic, or to pour concrete. We settled for clay and the work began.

The driver of the earth-mover was a large and casual man, and I watched, almost biting my nails with anxiety, as his huge scoop swung into the turf. We had trailed long pieces of white cord across the grass to indicate where the outlines of the pools should be. They looked inadequate and amateurish, but were in fact carefully worked out. To disturb the ground too close to the retaining wall might weaken it. And at the lower level there had to be a three-foot edging to the pool on each side in order to lay paving and walk round it. A narrower strip would have been uncomfortably close to the bottom of the retaining wall on one side, and to the oak pillars on the other. Amazingly, the casual driver could manipulate his scoop as neatly as a girl eating ice-cream with a teaspoon, and nearly as fast. Truckloads of subsoil, gravel and stones and all, were driven out through the field gate and dumped into a convenient hollow. Within two days we stood looking down into two alarmingly deep pits.

'Now for the clay,' said Mr Hatt, having also looked into them with reassuring approval. 'About a hundred tons should do it.'

In another exercise of astonishing accuracy huge quantities of blue rubbery clay were poured and shovelled into the holes, then pummelled and thumped into place. At this stage the depths of the pools had to be matched up with the levels, and there was a great deal of work with tapes, spirit levels and little sticks. The minimum thickness of clay to support water impermeably is about nine inches, and since the original ground levels were uneven this was not a simple matter like spreading butter on bread. But eventually it was done.

'Fine,' said Mr Hatt. 'Let me know when you're ready to think about circulating the water and I'll show you what to do. Good luck.' And off he went.

About this time the long spell of dry weather ended and World War One broke out.

I thought about pools that I had seen and could not imagine how to bring about the transformation of this battleground to any one of them, let alone two. Once Jack Hatt, with his fund of country lore and his breezy confidence, had deserted us, our faith wavered and was soon at a very low ebb. Rainwater collected in the ugly hollows and we were looking at deep

depressions in every sense. I supplemented the
rainwater from the garden tap, but all I could see then
was two huge cold puddles with ruts of shiny blue
clay across the bottoms of them. My power of
imagination died. There was one good week in
January when the ground was under snow and the
water was ice. In a white landscape only the outlines
remained and we could visualise the original plan
and were encouraged. Slush followed the snow, and
spirits sank once more.

Finally the ground began to dry out and in the late
spring we could start work again. There was no going
back, so we had to think of ways of going forward.
Malcolm and his partner, the other Malcolm, started
to level round the lower pool to make it ready for
paving. Paving-stones could not be laid directly on to
the clay, or they would merely slip into the water. The
Malcolms brought stones to support them vertically
and set the stones and the paving into cement. We had
a lucky and unforeseen source of stones for this job.
One of the small barns had a beautiful but broken
stable floor, similar to the floor of the orchard terrace.
Eventually it will have to be remade so that the barn
can be used again, but rather than waste the stones by
covering them we took up a great stack of them. Once
lifted, each stone resembled a large loaf of brown
bread. We laid a double row of them on their sides,
the tops of the loaves facing in towards the pool.
Pressed into the clay and then cemented, they made a
secure foundation for the paving-stones. There was
satisfaction, in fact excitement, in being able to find
such a use for the old stable floor.

If the men who laid those stones so skilfully
hundreds of years ago could see their time-warped
floor relaid round our ornamental pool in their old
cow byre, they might shake their heads in amazement

but not, I think, in disapproval. For me the old shapes edging the pool play a romantic part in the sequence of the years.

Now the lower pool was defined. Sixty feet long, and twenty across, oval at each end, it sat there uncompromisingly, waiting for me to work the magic.

THE LOWER POOL
In a bid for formality, this pool is edged with paving stones and the only planting is white waterlilies. They share the pool with a small lead fountain and a dozen brightly-coloured Japanese koi carp. The planting of the Golden Gate and its steps can be seen in front of the dovecot, and to the right is a shaggy silver willow-leaved pear.

Before we could attempt any planting round about, we had to import some topsoil. With acre upon acre of pasture stretching away across the wall, I felt foolish spending money on earth, but it had to be done. Topsoil is interesting stuff. Somebody else's discarded plants always come along with it. This load had snowdrops scattered through it and, less charmingly, sprouting potato plants here and there. However, it was good soil, and with it I made a narrow bed at the bottom of the retaining wall, in the space I had left alongside the paved edge of the pool.

If there are *Alchemilla mollis* anywhere in a garden there will be seedlings in the spring, and I collected enough to plant a row of them all along the bed. I was about to lift one or two large plants from the herbaceous border and divide them too, but Pat told me that seedlings will make far better plants and will fill the space as quickly.

I had only used alchemilla among other border plants before, but here I wanted to keep to green and lime-green only. In a continuous line and directly against stone, they look well, and the flowers overlap the paving just enough to soften its outline. If cut back as soon as they begin to turn brown, they will produce an even larger crop of flowers in late summer. The alchemillas echo the hellebores across the pool and against the opposite wall. Once in place these two rows are no trouble and only need occasional tidying.

Next to be planted were the six beams remaining from the cowshed. To start with I planted a vine, the common *Vitis vinifera* 'Brandt', at the bottom of each one. These vines have been dawdling, probably because of the soil where they are planted, but I am wary of their slothfulness and realise that they may well decide to move fast and furiously. When that happens they will need to be firmly shaped and held, or my restrained and architectural plans could be obscured in a massive tangle.

Apart from the vines, a different, tall-growing foreground plant is set against each pillar on the side that borders the pool. They were experimental choices, sharing two characteristics: they were to be 'sculptural' in shape and the only colours were to be variations of green and white and gold. On one pillar is a clump of macleaya with bronze plumes reaching to seven feet and with scalloped basal leaves. Against another is a fennel, not quite so tall, but also bronze, upright and feathery. A third has several *Acanthus spinosus* at its base, only rising to three feet but certainly entitled to inclusion in any grand sculptural plan. Next door to it is a *Spiraea arborea*, still on the same theme, and at the far end I have planted a golden hop, *Humulus lupulus* 'Aureus'. This may well get out of hand once its roots are well down, deciding to grow to fifteen feet or more, so I thought the last pillar would be the safest place for it. It can scramble over the end wall and off into the middle distance if it wants to, without getting in the way of anything else. It dies to the ground every year but makes vigorous growth in the summer.

There is one pillar that differs from the others in that there is a small well beside it with a low stone surround. Some years ago, before the pools were thought of, I planted a *Rosa* 'Macrantha' beside it as a promise, or at least a gesture, that one day I would concentrate on the sunken garden and its well. The rose grew up the pillar untended and one or two long sprays have drooped low so that in June the well is overflowing with clusters of small white roses. The effect is far too pretty to abandon for the sake of mere consistency, although pretty is not the key word for

ACANTHUS MOLLIS
Very handsome perennials. The purple and white spines of the flowers are statuesque and very welcome when most of the border is past its best in August. Acanthus mollis *and* Acanthus spinosus *do not differ greatly, but the difference is at once clear to a gardener who does not wear gloves.*

the lower pool's garden. To take the eye from the 'unsculptural' rose, I planted in front of it an extremely expensive, rather rare *Aralia elata* 'Variegata'. (The non-variegated aralia is, I believe, less expensive and more commonly found.) It is said to grow to about eight feet tall and has large, deeply cut, green and white leaves in elegant fans. It is also said to be easy to grow in most soils. Since mine grows at the rate of one inch per year and is now two feet high and four years old, I am reminded that the ground under the cowshed, that unattractive mixture of red clay and gravel, is not 'most soils'. Nevertheless, an aralia is an interesting, even exotic, little tree, with an original shape. In winter it turns into a very dead-looking, knobbly, twisted stick. However, I like it.

ARALIA ELATA VARIEGATA
This is not to be confused with the common aralia which is also called fatsia. Aralia elata *is an original little tree, and the 'variegata' means that its deeply-cut leaves are interestingly edged with white.*

While this planting was in progress, Malcolm turned
up one day with turf, and everything changed
instantly. Under the pillars was suddenly a long green
lawn the length of the hellebore wall and extending
to the pool's edge. At last we could see it in reality –
the formal pool with its paved border giving on to
grass, with an arcade behind it. As soon as one big
constructive step is taken in making a garden, every
remaining difficulty fades. One realises how to fill the
gaps which have been so awkward. Problem corners
tell you what they need, and tentative designs fall
decisively into place. I had thought of sowing grass
seed; and there is a delight in watching the delicate
greening-up of the ground. But I believe that the
advantage of laying turf is not merely that it satisfies
impatience. A suddenly changed view can jolt one's
mind into fresh ideas and perspectives. Spaces and
shapes that have been taken for granted may need to
be altered or used differently.

On this occasion, the grass laid along the pool
revealed the unusual nature of the walk between the
pillars and under the cross beams. That is, the cross
beams are low – one can easily reach up to touch
them – and the impression is of an unexpectedly
hidden grassy pathway – almost a tunnel. At present
this is only noticeable from inside, looking along the
beams, but when the vines grow tall they will
emphasise this impression and the walk will be quite
secret. On the wall behind the hellebore I have
planted four more vines, *Vitis vinifera* 'Purpurea',
which I hope will spread and mingle with the
green-leaved ones and enclose the space even more.
In early autumn their leaves, though purple against
the wall, are startlingly scarlet against the sky, and
bunches of small dark grapes hang on every branch.
Last of all, there is a *Garrya elliptica* on the furthest

wall, a fine dark-grey shrub with pale-grey winter catkins. This rounds off and finishes the garden.

Looking along the walk, we felt there was an obvious need for a thing – an artefact, a statue or an ornament – anyway a focus. Finally we decided on a Japanese stone lantern – a *toro* – whose distinctive shape now stands broodingly but considerately, with the grey garrya behind it. Considerately, because these *toros* are used in Japanese gardens to guide visitors by lighting their way up steps or round corners, as they go to the drinking fountain or the tea ceremony. There are a certain number of classic designs, all economical and symmetrical, and a small light can shine through them in each direction. The ancient moss-covered *toros* in temple gardens are often almost hidden, but they stand with great dignity and permanence in their appointed corners. Ours is one of the fine old shapes, but it is nevertheless new. I am encouraging the development of a suitably ageing patina by painting it over from a bucket of water strongly laced with cowpat. I hope it will come to appreciate the indignity when lichen begins to creep over its surface. Meanwhile, it brings a sense of proportion to the grass walk within the erstwhile cowshed.

GARRYA ELLIPTICA AND TORO
Toros have strong shapes and in Japan they are always placed in careful relation to plants or other stones, so that their dominance remains very discreet. My lantern, not yet mossy and ancient, is at least assisted in merging with the landscape by the spreading background of Garrya elliptica. The garrya's leaves are evergreen and dark, with heavy grey catkins drooping softly in February.

There are two ways by which one enters the lower pool garden. One was already defined by a simple arch of black iron. This is the Golden Gate that we erected in order to link that part of the garden with the orchard by another identical arch, the Pearly Gate, a hundred yards away. The other had to be created. By the time the digging and construction were complete, the further end of the lower pool was no longer on a level with the place behind the tithe barn. Instead of being able to walk through to it a steep bank downwards had to be negotiated. In a very few days Malcolm dug out a flight of half a dozen broad shallow steps using left-over paving stones for the treads, and more of our barn floor-stones as risers. The floor-stones make the steps look as though they have been there for a very long time. The only question is: what are they doing there at all? Possibly in the distant future archaeologists will form elaborate theories as to where such a flight of steps might have led and will dismiss as trivial the true answer (which is merely to enable one to get to the bottom of them, and then up again to the top).

I have already heard a pleasing explanation of the ponds themselves from a tourist peering over the dovecot wall. I was weeding at the foot of the Golden Gate arch, out of sight but within earshot of determinedly investigative tourists. One man was anxious to share his knowledge of domestic medieval life with the group of which he was the evident leader.

'There would often be a pond like this,' he told them, 'for the ducks, and to water the cattle and so on, in these old country places.' A voice slightly further away called out, 'There seems to be another pond close to it here. What about this one then? This one doesn't look like a duck pond.' A pause while the leader made his way to the next gap at the corner of

THE GOLDEN GATE AND THE CHURCH
The three climbers planted at the base of the Golden Gate are the roses
'Leverkusen' and 'Highfield', and Lonicera × tellmanniana. *The roses show a*
reluctance to behave like real climbers but the honeysuckle tries quite hard.
From the lower pool, this view leads the eye up three steps, over the grass,
past the granary, to the tower of St Kenelm's church.

the wall and thought about it. 'Ah yes,' he said. 'Well.
That would be an ornamental pool. This farm was
next to the big house so they would have been quite
sophisticated and had ornamental pools too.'

They passed on. I was left alone with a sense of
superb achievement. I had not only created a
recognisably medieval duck-pond in eighteen
months, but in my fifteenth-century sophistication I
had aspired to an ornamental lily pool as well. I was a
little embarrassed that the lady of the manor should
have had to pick her way across the cow byre and

round the duck-pond to reach her elegant pool and sit beside it with her maidens. But she might have forgotten the discomfort of her muddy feet if she had looked up at the retaining wall, where a youth would have been perfectly placed to strum on his lute, while his legs dangled above the *Alchemilla mollis*. My day was made.

Not until the clay and the paving and the turfing were complete could I think seriously about the water itself. Then I turned on the taps slowly and gradually the pools filled up. Being completely without vegetation they still looked disconcertingly shallow and bare. Cautiously I introduced a few handfuls of *Elodea crispa*, half a dozen more distinctive water plants, and seven waterlilies, cream ones for the lower pool, and pink and yellow for the top pool.

Shortly after this we bought some fish. There were nine golden orfe for the top pool, with six silver orfe alongside them. Orfe are just small wild fish, swimming in a little shoal, shy and indistinguishable one from another. Into the lower pool, to be ornamental and formal, we slipped ten Japanese koi carp. They are of various sizes and patterns, all completely distinctive in their wonderful colours and even their characters, so they are all individually recognisable. After a matter of weeks they would come nosing towards my fingers when I brought them a handful of strongly smelling food pellets. Having been scornful of fish-keeping I soon became devoted to the koi carp, though not to the extent of reading little chapters about their unattractive ailments which seem to be to do with constipation and various nasty infestations. It was, I now realise, well worth paying a good price for healthy fish in the first place.

Before long, however, our pretty fish became less and less visible and the water less and less clear. At first we relied on some convincing jargon about natural balances in water to reassure us. Then I heard about algae which cause discolouration when the temperature changes. Next I heard about clay ponds having to settle, and about oxygenating plants, and more about algae. So I determined to be patient and turned my attention instead to the planting round the upper pool. Water irises and bog primulas and moisture-loving plants of all kinds became possible for me for the first time. I read two or three water-garden books avidly, but decided not to be too ambitious in my first season. The more specialised water plants are in any case not easily available.

Having planted so much near the formal pool it had claimed my attention all through the spring, and the informality of the upper pool was becoming both an understatement and a challenge. My first puzzle was that when you build a clay-lined pool, the clay denies you a real bed for planting close to it. The few inches of topsoil that slope down into the clay are soon invaded by weeds and grass, and the single row of stones placed to hold a firm edge becomes partly submerged. The mower has no way of reaching right to the edge of the water. One has to have faith that the careful conditions of a herbaceous border are really unnecessary.

I started off trying to make proper holes for primulas but there is little to be gained by neatly laying young roots into rubbery blue clay, impenetrable to both soil and water. Before long I was reduced to tugging out clumps of grass and squishing the damp roots of my water plants into their place. After a slow start they spread themselves out and began to grow. Some, including a few hostas and a double white filipendula, stayed firmly on shore, while others, particularly the *Iris sibirica* and *Iris kaempferi* soon felt their way towards the water. The reeds of course spread right into the water, the best of them being the pretty pink-flowering rush called *butomus*. I avoided other rushes as being too invasive, but I did try two water grasses which have done well. I also decided against the very large decorative waterside plants such as rheum and gunnera, because they are so dominant, and found instead a small bog arum which marches charmingly into the water and has upright flowers, very white like small sails. Sections break off, attach themselves to various corners of the pool and march off again, but they are very easily controllable if they get too big for their boots.

Meanwhile the water itself was getting worse instead of better. It was cloudy and grey, and the *Elodea crispa* had become a solid sheet of dark-green chains, coated with a film of grey mud. The beastly stuff spread deeply through the muddy water and to make things worse the level of the upper pool began to fall. We never discovered where the leak was, but Mr Jack Hatt reappeared on the scene and helpfully cured it by spreading a yellow powdery compound called bentonite. This is a form of fuller's earth, designed to penetrate any crack or leak that could possibly appear. The main object of that exercise was achieved and there has never been any suspicion of another leak, even when I have detected moles burrowing perilously close to the edges.

But we still had muddy water, green chains, and shiny yellow sludge as well. I thought of the clear still pools of my dreams. By the time I had decided that all these problems had nothing to do with algae or 'natural balances', the autumn was upon us. Apart from some ineffectual grabbing at the elodea there was nothing more to be done until the winter had come and gone.

There had been one step forward during that season, however: we had established the circulation of water between the two pools. The height was there for a fall of water, but the connections had to be organised. First we lifted the largest single slab of stone that we could find in the garden. It had been laid in an old stretch of path and measured roughly three feet square. Malcolm took down a few layers of stone from the retaining wall and inserted this flat slab. Next he buried a four-foot length of four-inch pipe from the edge of the upper pool so that it reached the flat slab and rested on it. Then he built the wall up again. Now there was a lip jutting out from the wall and when the pond level was high enough the water ran through the pipe and across the big slab of stone. It fell about four feet down to the ground below at the far corner of the lower pool, about two yards from the ege.

Now it was my turn to take a hand, and I dug out a very small pool, about five feet across and a foot deep, lined it with a piece of black liner, and covered the liner with stones. A little tunnel led from it into the lower pool under the paved edge. Meanwhile, at the other end of the pools, a small electric pump took water back from the lower pool to return it to the upper one. So the circulation was completed with a small waterfall into the little pool that I had dug out.

This would all have been a very satisfactory state of affairs but for one crucial element – the water. The bottom of the pools had a mysterious layer of soft unsettled clay, nearly a foot deep, on top of the firm clay base. Several times I had tried siphoning out this layer while running clear water in on top, but that made very little impression. By the time spring came and the water began to warm up, the muddy green chains of elodea filled the water almost completely and I was at a loss. The vision had not materialised and the hard work was wasted. Time had had its chance and not proved to be the great healer as far as my ponds were concerned. It was impossible to judge the depth of solid clay; nor could we be certain whether one could tread on the bottom without either getting completely stuck or causing a leak.

So I bought a very small rubber dinghy. Feeling foolish, I pushed off into the middle of the upper pool and pulled out armfuls of chain weed. Fortunately this appealed to various members of the family, who were game for a couple of weekends of hilarious and energetic boat games, collecting bucketfuls of weed and mud, and hosing each other down afterwards. It was not, however, the answer.

One day, having switched off the pump and closed off the waterfall, I emptied the lower pool by siphoning the water away through two lengths of hosepipe. During two days we watched nervously for the carp lest they should get stranded in the mud. They must have been watching us even more nervously. Eventually we netted them all as the water diminished into puddles, and slipped them into the upper pool to join the orfe. We were left with the very unpleasant sight of thick grey soup, interlaced with the roots of the green weed, firmly gripping the clay below. At first we tried emptying it out with buckets, but that was completely beyond us. We had to borrow a monster vacuum cleaner called a slurry tanker. A most obliging neighbouring farmer lent it to us, sucked up the sludge and took it away to God knows where. There remained a reassuringly firm clay bottom over which we spread a few long boards so that we could walk across and pull out the worst of the remaining elodea roots.

The plan had been to cover the bottom with gravel but it seemed likely that the gravel would sink into the surface of the clay and the whole process might start again. As an insurance we spread a layer of very thin sheeting rather like fibreglass. It is not a liner but makes an effective barrier between the ground and a poured surface. Finally we spread the gravel, five tons of it, about two inches deep all the way across the pool, and slowly refilled it. The poor waterlilies had been languishing in mud for three days; they gasped with relief as they floated again and I washed their leaves clean. The water was divinely clear.

I thought the carp would come to my call and that I should be able to catch them and return them to their lovely fresh pool. But they had learnt wild ways from their visit to the orfes' pond, and anyway were not disposed to trust me after their traumatic experience with the draining of their own pool.

After a few weeks we were sufficiently recovered from our gruelling efforts to set about the same exercise in the upper pool, and completed the job in mid-July. The fish were thoroughly demoralised because they had to be caught again and put in a bath for three days. At least they were easily separated so as to be returned to their appropriate pools afterwards. Despite all my efforts, one little orfe slithered down the plughole to oblivion, but he was the only casualty. I had heard that carp easily become neurotic and I would not have been surprised if the shock had killed them. However, they all survived, although they were understandably wary and shy for several weeks afterwards, diving under the battered waterlily leaves at the sound of my footsteps instead of swimming up boldly to nibble round my fingers.

The two clear pools with a small sparkling waterfall between them were a joy and a source of amazement, after nearly two years of struggle. The gravel soon lost its slightly raw look and softened to a mild sandy colour.

The layer of soft mud and the murky suspension above it seem to have been peculiar to our pools for I have come across it nowhere else. I have my own theory to account for it, which is that most pools are either smaller and shallower, or larger and deeper. The smaller ones are made with stone or concrete or lined with plastic. The larger deeper ones, often older, have a greater weight of water to press down the clay, or even if there is a layer of suspended clay, it is too deep to be noticed and there is clear water above. I imagine that leaf humus and general detritus gradually accumulate and the water eventually filters clear.

I doubt if I shall ever really know what went wrong, but I feel I can take in my stride whatever horrors of water gardening may appear in the future, be they blanket weed, algae, cracks or floods. I also know that I shall never be guilty of complacency. I inspect the water for any sign of resurgence of the wicked green chain-weed, and if an occasional frond creeps up alongside the root of a waterlily it is pulled out in a trice. I know how quickly, for better or worse, any water plant will grow, and anything that could be described as invasive should be avoided like the plague.

The proportion of covered to exposed surface seems to be crucial to a pool, as is the presence of oxygenating plants of one kind or another. Waterlilies, which make good cover, are the only plants I want in the lower pool, to underline its formality and offset the mixed planting in and around the upper one. A small lead cherub now celebrates the clear water with a fountain in the lower pool. A useful cherub because he is oxygenating as well as charming.

IRIS PSEUDACORUS
Within the complex
classification of irises, this
one is unromantically
named a beardless
laevigatae. Its distinctive
shape and well-known
splash of gold make it
almost required planting
beside, or even in, a pool.

The challenge of planting the upper pool lay in its selective unsophistication. At one end a clump of kingcups with river mint, water forget-me-nots and the yellow flag, *Iris pseudacorus*, are quite separate from rushes, hostas, primulas and Japanese *Iris kaempferi* at the other. The pink and yellow waterlilies are more cheerful and less pure than the waxy white flowers of the lower pool. I did plant a pretty *Nymphoides peltata*, the 'Water Fringe', with well-shaped rounded leaves and neat yellow flowers standing out of the water, but it spread too fast, almost competing even with the elodea, so I had to take it out.

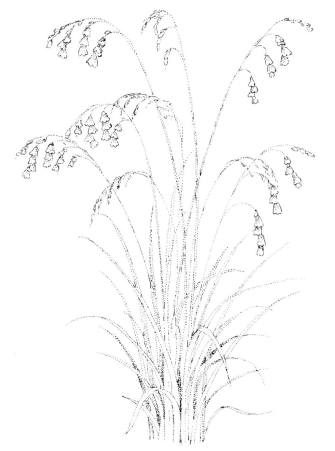

DIERAMA PULCHERRIMUM
This is also known as the 'Wand Flower' or more fancifully as 'Angel's Fishing-Rods'. Mine stand gracefully beside the pool. In late summer the weight of their flowers causes the stems to arch gracefully as though the angels had already hooked their slim pink fishes.

The tiny pool is my favourite because I dug it myself and because the waterfall drops into it. A couple of miniature ferns grow beside it, and one *Osmunda regalis* against the wall. A hart's-tongue fern that I scraped out of an Irish ditch grows in the wall itself, alongside a golden stonecrop. There is a variegated silver lamium, *L. maculatum* 'Beacon Silver' which needs to be kept under control, covering a few cracks, and a water speedwell spreading over the edge and into the water. There is no space for more planting there except for two 'Angel's fishing-rods' near the edge. These are properly known as *Dierama pulcherrimum*, and the less tall *Dierama pendulum*. Their flowers are pink, so they have no right to be in the sunken garden, but I broke the rules for them because I could not resist the opportunity of seeing their delicate wands against the waterfall.

A fine Sunday morning in summer means a drink on the terrace. A drink on the terrace means a time to survey the scene with a critical eye, a time when with luck one can see the wood for the trees. On one such morning I looked across at the upper pool, newly and happily planted, and was surprised by a sense of disappointment, a blankness in the view. There was, I realised, an expanse of grass between the pool and the barn that, although pleasantly smooth, was too unbroken and lacked interest. Heavy planting would have obscured the lines and diminished the space, but some height was needed. I already had two miniature willows, a woolly *Salix lanata*, and *Salix hastata* 'Wehrhahnii', close to that side of the pool so I decided that extending the theme of willows would only have relevance to water if I could find varieties of the right proportion. During the course of the season I picked up a rooted cutting at a plant sale which was labelled, 'a good small willow for the side of a pool.' I took a chance and it has proved to be just that. I think it is probably *Salix elaeagnos*. Later I saw, growing in another garden, a real beauty, silvery grey with very fine leaves, called *Salix exigua*, so I ordered one from Scott's. My little grove of willows had nearly become what I was seeking, but still needed one high point. Taller willows would have threatened to grow too broad so I had to look elsewhere. Then Pat thought of a silver birch and suggested the most silver-white of them, *Betula jacquemontii*. It stands behind the willows between the pool and the barn, with the fields and the sky behind it. Its shape promises well, and its bark is reaching its true colour. Very young silver birches have reddish-brown trunks almost like cherry trees. As they grow the thin-skinned outer bark splits away and the silver begins to show through. My *B. jacquemontii* started to do this at about four years old when tiny white triangles appeared at the angle of the trunk with each growing branch and the brown bark gradually peeled away. It is already a graceful little tree which will never be dense or give too much shade.

There is no more room for planting by the pools now, and I shall see the balance change with the years, as shrubs and vines mature. There are carp and a fountain instead of 'Four Ducks on a Pond'. We have had our traumas but I do not remember them with tears. Peter's insistence on pools, so alien to me at first, has been vindicated, and I find them endlessly interesting and pleasing. I see now that everyone needs a pool in their garden. However, I sometimes remind myself of the comment of a friend who came to visit me on the day work started on the pools. She enquired what was going on, and when I told her that I was embarking on water, she didn't say, 'How lovely' or 'What fun'. She is a very experienced gardener and she just said, 'How brave'.

8

The Rose Connection

(License my roving secateurs, and let them go . . .)

o here is the garden, and there is the orchard, and over there is the water and up there are the 'Nevadas'. But the whole thing is really the space one wanders about in. Each space makes its own demands; some ask for a permanent growing shape, others need plantings which wax and wane with the seasons. The old barns, for example, seem to shun the idea of planting; flowers and flowerbeds there would be out of place. They retain an eternal atmosphere of farm work which has endured over the centuries and on their walls even the most favourite climbers would look foreign.

So while individual areas retained their separate identity, it was nevertheless important to create a sense of continuity between them and to establish an awareness of the whole. To open doors, in fact; to connect.

The abiding spirits of Vita Sackville-West and Gertrude Jekyll and Robinson inspire gardeners today, and it is hard to imagine planting and the association of plants without accepting their influence. One of the concepts of those days was the creation of 'rooms' as part of a large garden. As I wander round the great garden at Hidcote in Gloucestershire whose creator, Lawrence Johnson, was a brilliant proponent of this design, I realise that my own garden, although not in the very slightest respect comparable, nevertheless needs the exactly opposite approach.

The house, the barns and the dovecot all have their own perspective in relation to the church and the Ruins and their connection has existed over a long period of time. They have a more tangible unity in space, and my corner of the space could easily have been fragmented by walls and angles, so I had to try to hold on to the unity. The garden itself, once planted, could easily have become a separate area shut away in a cul-de-sac. So I aimed at effects that would lead the eye, and indeed the feet, through the next gap and round the next corner. A seat under an apple tree on the lawn is a satisfactory place to take your book, but I believe the pleasure has an added dimension if you are just faintly aware of another seat beside the pools. It is not within calling distance but it might be worth moving there when the sun slips round the side of the church. And very much further away across the two fields one can catch a glimpse, between the barns, of picnickers beside the river. To shade off the divisions enhances a sense of flow between each part in relation to the next. And whatever my hit-and-miss efforts may be, the effortless simple continuity through fields, churchyard, Ruins and garden is the unifying and ubiquitous grass.

Designers and landscapers talk about installing 'permanent features' and planning round them. In my case the feature of the permanent features is their very permanence. Willingly accepting the dominance of the barns, I found I also accepted the various free-standing walls as immutable and intrinsic to the place. As indeed for the most part they are, and I work within the limits set by them. But once in a while a feature may be less permanent. Two years ago I undertook a very modest structural change and found that it completely revolutionised the place.

Across the garden, looking away from the house, is a wall, and beyond this wall are the croquet lawn and

the 'Nevada' roses. I used to think it a great pity that
the wall, being six feet high, hid the 'Nevadas' from
the garden. Indeed, we could only just glimpse
even the tall *filipes* and 'Bobbie James' roses on the
boundary wall behind the Nevadas. But, I continued
to think, we could not do without the wall because
the garden itself would lose definition – and anyway it
had always been there. Side by side these two
thoughts remained with me for years, so I would find
myself standing on my toes to look over the wall as
though into someone else's garden, or walking all the
way round the woodshed to reach the croquet lawn.

Then one day there arrived a whole new thought. I
would have called it lateral thinking except that I was
not thinking at the time: it just arrived. (Also Peter
Medawar, the author and medical scientist, once told
me that there is no such thing as lateral thinking.
There is thinking or not thinking. He must have done
more thinking than most people so I think he should
know.) In any event, my thought was this: lower the
wall. So, as you can see, it was an extremely small
thought. However, I still wonder why it did not come
to me years earlier and am still amazed at the
difference it made. The wall is now three feet high,
with a gap in it at the end near the summerhouse so
that one can walk through from the garden to the
'Nevadas', as well as being able to see them even from
the house. The flowerbed at the end of the garden
still has its background wall (an adequate three feet)
and my separation and continuity are simultaneously
achieved.

Next came an unexpected by-product. Instead of
being tucked away inaccessibly, the *filipes* and
'Bobbie James' roses were immediately accessible
from the garden, through the little gap in the lowered
wall. I looked at them more closely and realised how

meanly I had treated them. They were longing for
more height and the great shoots were falling off the
boundary wall, many of them damaged or wasted by
bending back on themselves. I wondered whether a
few stakes would help, but that would clearly be
inadequate. One day I decided to talk it over with
Malcolm and then wait for inspiration. But this is not
Malcolm's style; if he scents a project and approves of
it, he will sort out the necessary ingredients and get
on with it.

The very next week I arrived home to be
confronted with a great wooden structure, a sort of
medieval scaffolding. Two rows of ten-foot-high poles
in rough wood, eight feet apart and with connecting
crossbeams, were in place behind the 'Nevadas'. They
appeared to have no possible justification or use
(unless the electricity people were putting up new
cables again) and they were completely bare. My
heart sank, but Malcolm looked modestly proud and
as the things were firmly set in cement there was
nothing much to be said. I hid my misgivings and
turned to a discussion of the ever-fruitful subject of
composting.

But twenty feet is nothing to a *filipes* (especially the
'Kiftsgate' form) or a 'Bobbie James', and after some
balancing on ladders and tying-in of shoots they were
clearly prepared to climb up one side of the poles,
across the top and down the other side. Indeed, they
took it in their stride and after only one year we had a
great spread of July roses above our heads. Malcolm
shrugged as I enthused over the result of his project.
'Oh well,' he said, 'it keeps them out of the way of the
mower.' (Like children, 'off the streets'.)

So the beginning was functional but then I grew
ambitious and dreamed of walking under a longer
frame, a real colonnade of roses. (I use the word

colonnade because its height gives a more spacious and airy effect than a pergola, although it is not very wide.) We extended each end with more poles and now a 'Rambling Rector', a 'Paul's Himalayan Musk' and a *Rosa wichuraiana* will be equally tall neighbours to 'Bobbie James' and *filipes*.

One fly in the ointment and a very solid fact of life is a telegraph pole which stands at one end of our colonnade, conspicuously off-centre, boring and defiant. But not unchallenged: there is a plan.

Also at the same end of the colonnade, this time deliberate and central, stands Pierre. He is a French poet, five feet high. Being both stone and French and having arrived as a birthday present to Peter, he can only be Pierre. He has been moved to various places in the garden, looking for his ideal home (not very often because he is, for a poet, extremely heavy) and now we feel sure that the end of the rose colonnade is perfect, both for him and for the roses. Being such a romantic fellow he might well like to be associated with a column, an off-centre Grecian affair, not to be examined too closely, but from a distance or by moonlight it will not at all resemble a bit of moulding round a dreary telegraph pole. The idea is Peter's so the execution must be his one day. It is not exactly in line with the medieval Cotswold image, but this may be a moment to abandon consistency in favour of romance. A Folly for Pierre? We shall see.

This fortuitous piece of planning came late upon the scene. Earlier, we faced the problem of how to suggest a link between the orchard and the sunken garden (now the pools) across the intervening grass. There were already two eight-foot-wide openings in the connecting walls, each over rough and shallow steps of broken stone. They had probably once been gateways, but no gates remained. Pigs and poultry had been kept in the orchard, and the sunken garden would have been gated when cows were driven in there for milking. Without any livestock to be contained, the two openings were mere cessations of walls; negative gaps. We decided on arches and a blacksmith found no difficulty in erecting them. They are plain double bars of narrow black iron, eight feet high at the centre, with crossbars, so that they resemble curved ladders with widely spaced rungs. They certainly made a link where there had been none. To walk through one arch towards the other has become the natural route round the garden.

The new effect was unexpectedly strong, as was the wall-lowering exercise later, and we left it at that for a while. Then came the question of planting the arches and we looked for simultaneous differences and likenesses. Peter came up with the answer: they were to be the Golden Gate and the Pearly Gate, with planting to match, and it was for me to clothe his idea.

From the start the sunken garden was intended to be planted with a restricted colour scheme, so a Golden Gate would match that notion. Since gold and silver and greens were to predominate, there was no great difficulty with climbers. On one side I planted a 'Leverkusen' rose; on the other a rose called 'Highfield' and a bronze honeysuckle. The 'Leverkusen' must have been invented for little girls' birthday parties, or bridesmaids' posies. It is an exquisitely pretty pale yellow rose, semi-double with small frilly petals. It is glossy and healthy too, with no trace of mildew or blackspot, but not quite tall enough to reach the centre of the arch. 'Highfield' is strong too, and healthy, and also not quite tall enough, but in comparison with 'Leverkusen' it is coarse with thick rigid stems. The height I need comes only from the honeysuckle, *Lonicera × tellmanniana*. This is also rather coarse as honeysuckles go, but has a fine bronze flower and appealingly simple, almost primitive leaves behind each flower in a plain, thick green cup. On each side is a cornus. One is *C. alba* 'Elegantissima' and the other *C. alba* 'Spaethii', and between them the arch curves above four broad steps that lead down into the sunken garden.

ROSA 'LEVERKUSEN'
This is quite a recent rose and was raised by W. Kordes in Germany. The flowers are light yellow and daintily shaped, and its leaves remain glossy and healthy until the winter. Mine is about seven feet high, and if I were strong-minded enough to cut out some of the side-shoots, I dare say it would reach ten feet.

Next for the Pearly Gate. Having kept to the rules
with the Golden Gate, the design of the Pearly one
became something of a free-style jumble. Pale pink
and blue seemed fair choices, with a touch of white
for good measure; this was my nearest approximation
to Pearly. To start with I planted two roses; a 'Kathleen
Harrop', pale sister of the thornless 'Zéphirine
Drouhin', on one side, and a *centifolia* on the other.
Both are lovely pink roses and both of mine failed

*LONICERA × TELLMANNIANA
This honeysuckle was the
first to climb to the top of
our Golden Gate. The
strong, simple leaves form a
saucer round the handsome
bronze-gold flowers. It is less
delicate than other
honeysuckles but very useful
as a climber.*

hopelessly. 'Kathleen Harrop' still occasionally produces a few beautiful roses about two feet from the ground, but clearly hates her position. The bronze-green leaves of early summer do not live up to their healthy promise and succumb to blackspot before June is over. I ought not to have expected it to climb high, even at its best. The *centifolia* rose was a victim of premature senility and grew gnarled and twisted from the start. I hated to see such a fine rose so miserable, so I have taken it out.

It has been succeeded, in a hugely enlarged hole, by a 'Blairii No. 2' which I spray and feed and cosset because it has a bad reputation for mildew but is a great, old, full-pink rose. I have always wanted one, and it is not often to be found. Being on an open arch with plenty of air through it, I hope it will have a better chance against mildew than if it were against a wall. It is racing up the arch now, and intends to mingle at the top with a *Solanum crispum* from 'Kathleen Harrop's' side. The solanum is an uninspired climber with mauve potato-flowers in late summer. Mine is unfortunately not the 'Glasnevin Variety' which is a much better blue, but at least it is hardy and at least it climbs.

For a long time it seemed I had chosen roses with no head for heights to cover the arches. The fault was of course in my choice of rose. The reason for that choice was my anxiety that the arches should not be smothered and completely obscured by too much vigorous growth. Now that 'Blairii No. 2' is on the move I have probably over-reacted. Soon I may have to fight my way through the Pearly Gate with a machete, hacking at *Solanum crispum* on the left and 'Blairii' on the right.

The touch of white is supplied by a clematis, the beautiful large-flowered 'Marie Boisselot'. I hope she

CLEMATIS 'MARIE BOISSELOT'
My favourite of the pure
white hybrids, very
free-flowering. She is also
known as Mme. le Coultre.
Perhaps Marie married M. le
Coultre when she grew up?

won't feel threatened or suffocated by 'Blairii' and be
able to scramble across its strong shoots. Perhaps she
will glide – scrambling is too undignified an exercise
for such an aristocratic creature. She will certainly
add a touch of class to the solanum.

Now that the arches are finally settled, though not
mature, I am surprised at how difficult it has been to
establish successful planting. With hindsight I suspect
that I may have been up against the same problem
that arose in Arcadia.

Arcadia is a short walk along a row of five pillars
from which cross beams stretch to the wall that forms
the back of the orchard terrace. It is at right angles to

the house with the granary at one end, and an old woodshed (now a study), at the other. This was the site of the old tractor sheds whose black tin roofs we pulled off as soon as we moved into the house. The big square pillars and their beams undoubtedly had the makings of an arcade, though as supports they are crude and distinctly hefty. To sustain a more romantic vision than a deroofed tractor shed might conjure up, we christened it Arcadia and set about trying to plant it accordingly.

It was my first chance to indulge in climbing and rambling roses. The heavy pillars would be swathed in them and I prepared the ground eagerly. I wanted single flowers on long sprays, so in went a 'Frühlingsgold', a 'Frühlingsmorgen' and a *paulii* 'Rosea' whose petals are like heart-shaped confetti and change from pink with golden stamens to cream with brown stamens – a most endearing rose. Then a 'Meg' at the furthest end adjoining the granary and the pale and fragrant honeysuckle called 'Halliana'. The theme was a shading of pinks and yellows and the intention was to lighten the framework. Nearest to the house I planted a *Rosa moyesii*. Since its clear red flowers appear before all the others it need not fit the theme. Like *R. xanthina*, the 'Canary Bird' rose, it opens the season in its original and welcoming way.

The honeysuckle flourished, being a very undemanding sort of plant. The *moyesii* did well too, but after its very first flowering I conscientiously dead-headed it, not knowing about its marvellous hips. Even Pat, always constructive, winced when I told her, and for once was at a loss to detect a bright side to my ignorant action. Perhaps too, it is why my *moyesii* has never produced a hip in the whole of its life so far.

All the other roses deeply resented being there,

and sulked along slowly for about four years. Looking at the ground more closely, I realised that because the poor things were planted at the edge of a tractor shed the ground would always have been oily and trodden and it would of course never have been cultivated. Patches of dirty soil may be common to any number of edges and corners in a farmyard. A farmer carrying a bucket of disinfectant or a tin of creosote across the yard would naturally put it down to open or close a gate. Once in a while it might get knocked, or kicked over, or spilled by a jumping dog. The farmer's predecessors would have carried their earlier tarry equivalents in the very same way, their ghostly dogs jumping too, and over the years the ground would become impregnated with all kinds of substances. I was not expected to come along with my fancy ideas and plans, so it is not surprising that the soil beside these gateposts and pillars and farmyard corners is unfriendly to my precious roses. Between my dream and the reality these phantom farmers have ensured that a great deal of work and patience should intervene.

So the unhappy 'Frühlings' roses gave place to a young climbing 'Lady Hillingdon' and an 'Elegance', which went into very much larger holes with great dollops of compost, manure and bonemeal. Determined to get some action fast I invested in a *filipes* and an energetic clustering climber called 'Wedding Day'. These, once started, make short work of covering pillars, beams and anything else that comes to hand, and with the 'Halliana' honeysuckle the two of them take care of the far end of Arcadia. Since they flower late in July I hope it is not too obvious that their presence is attributable to my impatience rather than to any systematic design.

Arcadia and the Gates, both golden and pearly, were
useful concepts – apart from being images which
amused us. They served to keep our visions intact and
to help us make the essential link between one part of
the garden and the other.

When I started planning, I feared that the different
styles in each individual area would clash with one
another and that I would end up with a garden of
mixed assortments. Happily, it gradually became clear
that, on the contrary, the different elements
complemented one another. Arcadia, the Gates and
the Colonnade are the connections between them,
and I feel that if they have been successful, it is
because there was one overall unifying element at
work. Quite simply, the rose.

9

Family Feelings

A liking for one particular group of plants is mysteriously personal. It is more than popularity and different from taste, and it grows as familiarity grows. I was first struck by the pleasure in getting to know the various members of a plant family when I started to find out about geraniums (by which I mean the herbaceous geraniums, the cranesbills).

The first geraniums that I used were *G. endressii* 'Wargrave Pink', and *G. pratense* 'Johnson's Blue'. I was then given a small root of *G. sanguineum lancastriense*, and looked up geraniums in Graham Stuart Thomas's *Perennial Garden Plants*. He lists them on no less than six sides of a page, and as I read about more and more species and their varieties, the wealth of the geranium family began to dawn on me.

GERANIUM PRATENSE
A member of the widespread and obliging family of herbaceous geraniums. This one is the Meadow Cranesbill, native to Great Britain and Europe, and has itself parented many hybrid variations.

It is not only their great number that is interesting; it is the fact that there is a different plant for every conceivable situation. Their colours may be strong or pale, their flowers early or late, and the plants tall or creeping, bushy or narrow in outline. Some, like *G. sanguineum lancastriense*, make low clumps for the front of a border, but if that is too vigorous the miniature variety called G. × 'Ballerina' is of a similar size, although slighter – and even prettier. There is a big group, very hardy and easy to cultivate, that makes excellent ground cover. They include *G. endressii*, *G. pratense*, in particular 'Johnson's Blue', and many more.

In my early days of herbaceous planting they obligingly filled daunting patches of bare earth for me while other perennials were slower to establish. If they have a fault, it is that they can be too enthusiastic in their growth and have to be reduced from time to time. Some varieties have a short flowering season, and make up for this by recurrent lesser flowering late into the autumn. I am particularly fond of the double white form of *G. pratense*, which grows very fast and upright on light green stems and also seeds itself freely. It is one of the group that only flowers for a short time, but if I cut its flowered stems to the ground, they start all over again in a few weeks, so in fact they are very good value. Another lovely species, which is distinctive and will flourish in deep shade, is *G. phaeum*. It is also known as the 'Widow', and does have a gently mourning effect. It grows to about two and a half feet with deeply-cut leaves and many small near-black flowers. The geraniums in general give an invaluable impression of summery abundance in any garden, each variety contributing in its different way.

People can, and do, get deeply involved with the hosta family. New varieties appear every year, and their shapes and colours are endlessly improved upon. The trick seems to be to get exactly the right hosta into the right corner, when the result is very satisfying. Unfortunately, with the first inkling of ground frost, hostas suddenly stop trying, lie down in a limp heap and vanish. They justify their existence all over again in late spring when you can watch them grow from day to day as they unfurl fast and cleanly, coming strongly out of the bare ground. I think of hostas as necessary and useful and I admire them, but I don't feel particularly fond of them.

I started to grow paeonies about five years ago, and realised that this is a great mine to work. The *officinalis* paeonies that I found already growing in the garden were really the first ones I had looked at. When I read Kelway's catalogue with their collection of almost a hundred varieties, I was faced with an orgy and expected to fall in love with them. They couldn't be dotted about the borders in any great profusion because they are so dominant. I selected about a dozen eventually, feeling like a child asked to choose from a whole table of cream cakes. They vary between single and double, early and late flowering – a whole jumble of colours; and apart from one or two in the border I gave them a bed to themselves. Nearly to themselves; they share it with a *Spiraea* × *arguta* which is well past flowering when they come into their own, and which is cool against their richness. Rashly, I also planted a tree paeony at each end of the pump bed. They are marvellous plants but small as yet, although goodness knows how much space they may eventually commandeer.

I love the wealth the paeonies bring to the garden in June and July, but for some reason I feel no real affection for them. 'I like that pink one with the gold stamens', is how I think about a paeony, rather than knowing each one individually by its name. Looking at the catalogue lists, however, I wonder if I am making a great mistake. It appeals to me to find that elegant and high-born Ladies like 'Cornelia Shaylor' and 'Lady Alexander Duff' are jostling against the formidable 'Inspecteur Lavergne' beside 'Bunker Hill', while 'Lord Kitchener' leans towards 'Beersheba'. Nevertheless, I don't know which is which, and am not really aware of separate personalities in them. The tree paeonies are different and impressive, and I do know their names, which are 'Souvenir de Maxime Cornu' and 'Duchess of Marlborough'. One other exception is a lovely Japanese species paeony called *P. mlokosewitschii*. It grows to only eighteen inches or so, and takes a long time to flower. It has rounded leaves of a soft green, and pure pale yellow single flowers. I grow it in a herbaceous border with the darker green behind it of later-flowering phlox.

Pansies do have distinct personalities, but although I love each one, (as who does not?) it would rarely occur to me to know the name of a particular pansy. Love them, that is, provided they are grown separately. The beauty of any individual plant will be ruined in the mass. I believe this applies to every plant in cultivation, though not, as Wordsworth immortally noticed, in nature. A glimpse of his daffodils, or of a sheet of wild bluebells, has a quality which, however elusive, is instantly recognisable as the very opposite of deliberate massed planting. Wordsworth, lucky man, never saw regiments of pansies bedded out on roundabouts. If he had, his heart would surely have bled for them. Fortunately I have so many corners, angles, edges and crevices and

PAEONIA MLOKOSEWITSCHII
A less vigorous paeony than the big lactiflora hybrids. It is the earliest possible paeony to bloom in my garden, with a short flowering season. Both the yellow cupped flowers and the pale green leaves are soft and rounded. My favourite among paeonies.

so on in my garden that I can use pansies all over the place like minor punctuation marks.

The salvias are a family whose members are recognisably related to one another, and yet it is fascinating to seek out completely different forms to suit both one's needs and one's taste. The various sages are superb near the front of a wide curving border. The ordinary sage, *S. officinalis*, is a good plant, and the variegated ones are all beautiful. They do get a bit woody and straggly after some years and may grow out of bounds. But they will start again quickly from cuttings in a cold frame and sometimes will stand being cut hard back, shooting from the old wood. The purple one flowers particularly well, rather like a large ajuga, and its upright flower stems last for months.

I like to keep one or two tall *Salvia turkestanica* in the border. Its flowers are a pale mixture of blue and pink above woolly silvery foliage, giving a soft misty effect among stronger colours. Mine comes and goes from time to time, being a rather unreliable perennial. There are other good salvias, but my favourite is *S. sclarea*, the common clary. I saved a packet of seeds once and since then clary plants have been turning up, not only in the herb bed where they were originally sown, but all over the garden. Since they have decided to seed themselves I have discovered that they are particularly charming when they stand alone. If I come across one of the little rough-leaved seedlings in May I can move it to a place where it will look good, but of course there is no way of telling the colour of the flower beforehand, since they may be pink, blue or purple. A single branching plant may grow two feet high and nearly as wide. The best colour is in the top leaves, not in the flowers, so they last well into autumn.

My favourite plants are not all family groups; I have a few individual plants that I treasure beyond the others.

One is 'Bill Mackenzie'. He is *Clematis orientalis* 'Bill Mackenzie', named for the famous Wisley gardener. I bought it for a narrow area of wall, only one storey high, outside the French windows that open from the kitchen on to the terrace. A neat place, I thought, for some neat little yellow lanterns to nod, and I took out one paving stone to accommodate its root. Within two years 'Bill' had not only covered that wall, plus the wall round the corner and the nearby window, but had flooded across the terrace floor. This could have been annoying in a less attractive plant, but 'Bill's' enchanting flowers come in amazing profusion from June to October. By July it is showing its special conjuring trick – the whole spectrum appears simultaneously from the tiniest buds, through the opening, and then fully opened golden lanterns, to the exquisite seed heads. I cannot tell whether mine is a particularly rampant plant of its type, or whether I should have expected such vigour. Had I known, I would have offered it more space elsewhere. But it may be the combination of a southfacing wall and the fact that the roots run under the stone terrace which make it particularly happy. Perhaps it would not have thrived so well elsewhere. It is certainly a delightful neighbour when we sit on the terrace, and we do not grudge it the window. I cut all its stems to within eighteen inches of the ground

CLEMATIS ORIENTALIS 'BILL McKENZIE' This is a deluxe and larger-flowered version of C. orientalis. Cut almost to the ground at the end of winter, it will race energetically upwards through the early summer months. By July it will easily reach twenty feet, defying all plans to control or subdue its beautiful tangle.

in March. February is, I know, the recommended time but I trim a lot off in November for the sake of tidiness, and have to leave about half the dead growth across the window until March for the sake of a wood mouse.

When the weather gets cold this mouse takes over the outside of the windowsill for his winter quarters. He collects hundreds of seed heads, chews off the ends and spits them out, then weaves the soft bits into a big feathery ball to make his house. It is light and warm as swans-down with a little round hole on one side. The tangled clematis stems are a safe curtain from the owls, and the house wall must be warmer than the outside world. Not only is he safe and warm, but fed and exercised too. He eats the actual clematis seeds and on mild days scampers about in the framework of stems. He has chosen a perfect home, and we in turn can watch him through the windowpane. By March, when I see him less often, I cut the clematis right down and sweep away nest and all. Enchanting as it is, the mouse is not invited to be a permanent lodger to the extent of raising a family on the windowsill. The real favourite is 'Bill Mackenzie's' clematis, with the mouse a bonus, a poor second.

Most of my favourites have, or once had, an element of surprise in them. 'Bill Mackenzie' certainly surprised me, and I have not seen an identical plant growing in quite that astonishing way. I have had a passion for *Helleborus orientalis* since the first day I saw one. My very first planting order included four of them, on Pat's advice, and I had no idea what treasure to expect. I have since found the dark reds and pinks of the open flowers, with their streaked and spotted markings, more beautiful than almost any other flower; and the creamy white ones with green or pinkish markings the most beautiful of all. Every plant is different from the next, and although they can be recognised as distinct varieties, I am not sure which I can accurately claim to identify. I have one that is a soft yellow but whether it is a new strain from Miss Strangman's nursery where it came from, or whether it is the rare *H. orientalis kochii*, I cannot say. A few of the dark pink ones make seedlings, and these have their own tiny variations of colour. They are all hardy and reliable, budding on through the coldest winters well into spring, subtle and graceful.

You could almost call the *Helleborus orientalis* a family in itself, but *Cosmos atrosanguineus*, another favourite, is nearly alone. It is a perennial whose neat full rosette of leaves does not even venture above ground until May. In August and September it bears single flowers of darkest velvety red on narrow upright stems. The open cups of the flowers are very simple, and smell strongly of hot chocolate. I have two plants, each about eighteen inches high and a foot across. They are near to each other and also to three different cistuses, so the whole lot are rather tender. The cistuses let me know at once by their unhappy-looking twigs if the winter has been too much for them, but the cosmos might just not reappear. It is always a relief to see their shoots again in May. Their only immediate relation is the annual cosmos daisy, a very inferior and hoydenish cousin.

Each season has its best moments, and when one favourite fades, another is always on the way. Small bulbs are not of course a family, but there are treasures among them. Our snowdrops are inherited, and are nearly all double. I am devoted to them because they were so welcoming and unexpected in our first spring, and so profusely scattered. The snob in me ought to scorn them – I know Vita Sackville-West would not have allowed a double snowdrop within five miles of Sissinghurst. When I look at the pure single ones I understand that, but if you don't insist on a direct comparison the double ones are lovely little things in their own right.

Our inherited bluebells, on the other hand, also growing plentifully and casually, are by no means favourites of mine. They seem to me to be distinctly corrupted by their contact with civilisation. They are thick-stemmed and coarse, as though they would really prefer to be hyacinths. There is no romance in them and I have scrapped all but a very tenacious few. Their bulbs can be more than a foot deep, and hard to uproot. Perhaps the garden bluebell is only a distant relative of the woodland one, but domestication has not improved it.

Tiny bulbs are easy favourites and rarely present any problems. Every year I fall for a few more from the catalogues, and there is always a corner for a little scatter of *Iris reticulata* or *Iris histrioides*, scilla, or, more subtly, the starry ipheion. Or perhaps a species tulip. Of these, I have been lucky with *Tulipa turkestanica*, which has a thin and curling leaf and a creamy restrained flower. Although they are not conspicuous, a few of them together make a pretty and original shape, blooming early in the season.

In theory I love the dashing reds and yellows of species tulips, but in practice I have not found a natural home for them. I did plant a dozen of *T. Hageri* a few years ago and unfortunately they made an all too natural home for themselves. Having

TULIPA TURKESTANICA
This species tulip flowers in March and does not pretend to a striking or colourful display. In my garden it is the first plant of the year to have the self-confidence to be subtle. The flowers, several on a stem, are creamy understated stars. They stand about eight inches high above narrow grey-green leaves that curl outwards. They show themselves off well in small clumps.

flowered only once, they now send up hundreds of small leaves from bulbils year after year, mixed inextricably with other plants, and with never a flower to be seen. Possibly, however, they are growing from seed and before long I shall have a whole new generation of *T. Hageri* coming into flower. I rather hope not because then I should be obliged to feel proud of them, and they are not at all well placed.

I have tried to grow fritillaries from seed but I believe they are hard to grow and take many years to mature enough to flower. Apart from the ordinary *Fritillaria meleagris* which is lovely and comparatively easy, and which lives under my silver-birch, I have occasionally been tempted – after the Chelsea Spring Show – to buy one or two ravishing bulbs in flower. I would love to have a real collection of different fritillaries, but that must be for the professionals.

One more small bulb I like to have is the gold *Iris danfordiae*, brilliant and chubby, but I have found it is no good expecting it to come back reliably, let alone increase, so I now treat it as an annual and put in a few each year. Its brother, the *Iris reticulata*, on the other hand, is very long-lived and does increase. I have one dark purple drift of them on a small slope, with the *danfordiae* planted alongside, and I call them the Assyrians. Not that they come down like a wolf on the fold but their cohorts are gleaming in purple and gold to a height of at least three inches.

The big tulips are not very long-lived but at least they survive for three or four years. I have only one clump that I take seriously and restock whenever they threaten to diminish. (This is an admission of lazy gardening. I know full well that I ought to lift and replant them.) These are 'White Triumphator', a very tall lily-flowered tulip. I planted them closely in front

FRITILLARIA MELEAGRIS
The Snake's Head Lilies look their best in grass which is their natural meadow habitat. But their narrow leaves die down slowly while you wait impatiently to cut the grass. In most groupings there are a few white ones, a lovely variation on the mysterious mottled purples. The little knobbly bulbs are best planted on their sides so that the rain cannot penetrate their delicate crowns and make them liable to rot.

of a *Spiraea × arguta*, and happily the delicate, frothy white sprays of the spiraea come into bloom and hang over the 'Triumphator' at exactly the same time as the strong clean-lined tulips open up towards them. This was a chance success that made me realise for the first time the importance of precise timing in associations of plants.

And of course there is the daffodil family. Whether you look through the pages of a big catalogue like de Jager of Kent or study a smaller, more specialised grower like Avon Bulbs, the variety of daffodils and narcissi is irresistible. A neat clump, twelve-inches high, optimistically named 'February Silver' a few feet away from another of 'February Gold' (I have never known them to flower before mid-March) is a marvellous start to the season. I never mix varieties in planting but there is a great pleasure in walking all over the garden during March and April and bringing in from sloping banks and from under trees a handful each of twenty or more varieties to fill the house.

The season for the tall daffodils does spread over six weeks or more, and I have chosen the early ones from among the strong gold varieties, 'St Keverne', 'Dutch Master', 'Unsurpassable' and 'Carlton'. They are the great signals of spring that

> come before the swallow dares
> and take the winds of March with beauty.

But they are not an easy colour, and after the delight of the first week or so, I begin to perceive the gold as yellow, even eggy, and my eye takes a more sophisticated view. Then is the time to become choosy and the tempting catalogues prove their worth. The cream, the lemony, the bicolour, the pure white and the doubles all come into their own.

Among my favourites are 'Daydream', 'Irene Copeland', 'Desdemona', 'White Lion', the shaggy 'Telemonious Plenus', and the beautiful 'Tresamble'.

The tiny daffodils live in a world of their own, their leaders for me being 'April Tears' and even smaller 'Minnow', with 'Tête-à-Tête' hardly taller. They need to bloom in relation to their own environment or they will be in danger of just becoming insignificant instead of looking adorable. The places where cyclamen are happiest suit the miniature daffodils too – between the roots of a tree or under a still-bare shrub with no immediate competition. Even crocuses can look coarse alongside them.

I have found that the daffodils which are the closest to the wild plant can be quite slow to establish. I remember them blooming for mile after mile in the sunlit woods of Fontainebleau near Paris, where we used to have Easter picnics as children. To remind me of those incomparable woods I planted some 'Jack Snipe', which are presumably highly-cultivated but of similar dimensions to the true wild daffodil. They are in a wild patch near the dovecot where they are beginning to look less tentative and more at home. Recently, however, they received an unkind psychological shock from a passing workman. Beside the churchyard gate I sometimes dig in a few sturdy plants or bulbs that might withstand the casually-parked bicycles of local lads on their way to the river and also hide our dustbins from churchgoers. A clutch of strong 'King Alfred' daffodils grows there and the passing workman, catching my eye, said: 'You've a few daffs there, then.'

'Yes.'

'You know what *you* want?'

'No?'

'You want a few more.'

'JACK SNIPE'
This is one of the Narcissus cyclamineus *group, and is only eight inches high. The trumpet is yellow and the creamy perianth is swept back, reminding me of Piglet's ears 'streaming in the wind'!*

'I suppose so.'

'I tell you what, then.'

'What?'

'There's a few growing behind the dovecot I seen. Small miserable little buggers. No one wouldn't miss 'em if you dug 'em up and brought 'em round. They might grow properly here and wouldn't cost you.'

So much for 'Jack Snipe' and my childhood memories of romantic woodland picnics.

With daffodils, there is of course a price to pay – after their flowering we have to resist cutting the leaves for a couple of months. Our naturalised daffodils grow in very weedy grass and while it is uncut the thistles and docks grow maddeningly, even starting to seed. The cowparsley is at least a pretty compensation. The daffodils themselves are now rather weak-flowering and would probably benefit from dividing and feeding. But dividing is a near-impossible job in that stony ground, and the school of thought that recommends foliar feeding after bulbs flower must apply only to very clean planting. It is an absurd exercise to spray daffodil leaves with a nourishing liquid that is rejected by those waterproofed swords only to run straight on to the broad-leaved weeds, which lick their lips and flourish. I shall take the lazy way, which is to wait for the survival of the fittest. If the bulbs dwindle I shall allow them to fade year by year and then find a fresh wood for them, and pastures new.

Bulbs in general have proved more of a problem than I expected. Their foliage can be infuriating whether in grass or in beds, and it can take literally months to be clear of floppy dying leaves. Each year I

determine to lift some of the groups of daffodils out
of the flowerbeds and replant them, but as soon as
their flowering season is over, there are a thousand
distractions as spring advances, and the job loses its
priority. My best-placed groups are well back in the
borders, close to plants like catmint or geranium that
will begin to grow fast and bushily by the end of May,
obscuring the daffodil leaves completely.

ANEMONE PULSATILLA
These appealing purple
flowers with golden stamens
form twelve-inch-high
clumps. Their most attractive
feature is that they are
covered with fine silky hairs
and after flowering they
leave a bonus of silvery
round seedheads.

Some of my favourite plants have a special quality to them; the sculptured low-growing carlina thistle with its steely spikes and soft pure white seedheads ripening in its wide centre; the exotically pretty *Anemone pulsatilla*; the tender lemon-scented verbena, *Lippia citriodora*, which I grow in an urn and protect in the winter. But this is not always the case. I can think of two plants which are far from special and without which my garden would not *be* my garden. One is the heartsease that seeds itself all over the orchard terrace and crops up in any odd corner. I have never planted one and have destroyed many, usually by mistake in the course of weeding. The other, also a wild flower, is the foxglove.

For all my eagerness to become acquainted with new plants, and to learn which to grow and how to grow them, the one I needed no telling about was the foxglove. It embodies the country for me, whether in the wild or in a garden, and it was the first flower I looked for when we arrived. Not finding it, I went at once to the garden centres, carried home six specimens and planted them rather furtively: foxgloves should appear spontaneously, not be bought or planted. Mine were poor objects that had been pushed into a back corner in their plastic containers, and were almost dried out. But I have never had to buy another and now there are pools of seedlings to draw on each year. They are most accommodating to cultivate, and can be moved at any stage from tiny seedlings to leafy second-year plants. As they are biennials, it is worth placing large and small together, and I have plenty spreading naturally round the edges of the garden, so I will never be without them. A few are deliberately placed, especially white ones which are very stately in a border, but mostly they choose their own homes.

Each year one or two will appear somewhere
unexpectedly and alone, insisting on an emphasis
which will alter the whole line of a bed or a terrace. I
love them. I think of them in the same category as
owls, wild but with an imagined potential for
friendliness on their own terms.

I can rarely find it in my heart to love an annual but
there are one or two packets of seeds that I look
forward to sowing each spring. One is red flax, very
like its perennial blue cousin, *Linum perenne*, with
little clear flowers nodding above fine delicate stems.
The red flowers are somewhat more open and
upward-facing than the blue, and their great charm is
their satiny texture and pure cherry-red colour,
bordered with an almost invisibly narrow, darker
edge. They flower through July and August, closing at
sundown and opening again in the mornings. Taking
up practically no space in the ground they add
brightness and lightness to a herbaceous border.

My second packet of seeds is *Lavatera* 'Mont Blanc',
the annual white mallow. I start them on the
windowsill each in its own small pot, and put them
out singly in early May. Singly because each grows
into a handsome bushy plant, two feet high and nearly
as much across, with snowy-white flowers on strong
stems. They keep blooming over a long season, and as
night falls they gleam across the garden. They have
this appealing quality of white flowers that while
others, the reds, and the pinks and the blues, merge
into the dusk, they glimmer as though they were
themselves a soft source of light. Tall white daisies
float on approaching darkness, and white
delphiniums stand like faint torches as night gathers.

Whenever I am choosing plants, I am tempted by white forms if they are available; the white phlox, the white paeonies, white dicentra and white pinks – they and many others all have a romantic flavour that appeals to me more than the coloured varieties, and they are very often superior as plants too.

White roses, of course. (Unless, in the case of roses, I happen to be looking at a pink or a red or a yellow one.) But roses inhabit a world of their own, and are on a different plane from other flowers. They are a race rather than a family, and cover such a span of form and habits that favourites can only be chosen arbitrarily and with much qualification. Many gardeners, and I am one such, are addicted to the old shrub roses, the species roses and their hybrids. The Bourbons, the *gallicas*, and the Albas in my rose circle are certainly at the heart of my garden and I would give them pride of place anywhere. Outside the circle, apart from the 'Nevadas' and the climbers, are a few that have their own separate places. One is 'Buff Beauty', a hybrid musk rose that grows on the terrace near *Clematis orientalis* 'Bill Mackenzie'. It bears soft, many-petalled apricot clusters that hang down in a melancholy way. On either side of the entrance to the garden from the drive stand 'Mme Hardy' and *Rosa virginiana* 'Plena'. 'Mme Hardy' is a well-known Damask beauty with quartered blooms of a pure white which are enhanced by a tiny green centre. *Rosa virginiana* 'Plena', which is also called *R.* 'Rose d'Amour', is less well-known and has small pink flowers which open in a slight whorl. It is particularly lovely in bud when the long green frilly sepals cross over the emerging pink petals. The effect, like the name, is most romantic, unless it happens to remind you of over-pretty nursery wallpaper.

But even roses are subject to taste. I have no great feeling of affection for Hybrid-tea roses despite their perfection. I find their colours and textures often too harsh and obvious, and their habits too rigid.

The question of taste in gardening is subtle and by no means easy to define. It must grow from our personal preferences and perceptions and not be subject to transient changes of fashion. Everyone thinks their own taste is axiomatically good and that other people's taste is good insofar as it relates to their own. There are areas where 'good taste' shades into snobbishness and I have to own up to prejudice against a certain, fairly short, list of plants that come into my 'wouldn't be seen dead with' category. They are mostly the more garish bedding plants, the clarkias, the tagetes, the asters. I also include statice (sea lavender is such an unpleasantly salty image), chrysanthemums, laburnum and rhododendrons; while at the top of the list are dahlias. In my own defence, I would say that my list gets gradually shorter as my eyes are opened to previously-scorned treasures.

For instance, African marigolds are often used in this country as crowded formless blobs, their crude colours appearing even cruder in close proximity to mixed planting. But I once saw the very tall variety of African marigolds planted close to the grey trunks of palm trees in a garden in India. The trees themselves were widely spaced in grass, and the brilliant marigolds were finishing touches to a clean simple design. They would be no use in my garden, but I have at least learned to respect them.

I received one other forceful lesson in gardening taste (or was it in snobbishness), but I am not quite sure what I learnt from it. I took a friend of mine to see the rose circle. It was late June and the roses were at their best. Heavy sprays of 'Fantin-Latour' were bending to the ground. The youngest addition to the circle, the hybrid 'Roger Lambelin', had only three blooms but they were perfect; hundreds of flat petals of deepest crimson beautifully shaped, and with the crinkly edges touched here and there with tiny flecks of white. My friend loved the old roses, many of which she knew, and I loved her appreciation of them. A very satisfactory visit. Then we came to 'Roger Lambelin' and she stopped to look at it closely. 'What's this one?' she asked. 'It's perfectly beautiful. It's almost like a dahlia.'

10

Gardening:

Doing It and Reading About It
'Il faut cultiver notre jardin.'
Voltaire

he truth is that gardeners love gardening. Yet there is a particular variety of garden writer – a subspecies I expect, and certainly a perennial – who appears not to have grasped this vital point. 'Don't plant that one,' they say, 'it will need pruning.' 'Avoid so-and-so, you might have to water it.' I can imagine their own gardens: acres of ground smothered with impenetrable mats of dark green periwinkle. They never mention the joy of doing the actual gardening, which overrides every discomfort and disappointment.

I admit that I had not the slightest idea of how much work I was committing myself to as I began to plant up more and more of my garden. One day I suppose I shall have to simplify, to reduce the work, but until that day comes I can indulge in the satisfaction and absorption that is like no other activity in the world. Although I must confess that for the first two seasons there was nothing in an hour's or a day's work that merited the name of gardening. Digging my way round, I filled my wheelbarrow not with dear little weeds but with rusty barbed wire, with unearthed empty cans of hoof ointment, and other attendant constituents of farm life; some even less attractive. But these were small items to be cleared away among the expanses of stony rubble, and of course there were always the nettles which love fallen stone. Chasing the tough knots of their pink and yellow roots is one of the most engrossing jobs of coarse gardening. Feeling and prodding into the ground with a fork, you can even recognise them by their distinctive smell, and I used to drag out great handfuls of next year's trouble. If in the course of unravelling you are brought up short by a wall, you can be sure the nettles will be creeping back through the crevices by next spring. For years the battle goes on, sometimes spraying the young leaf, sometimes grubbing out the old roots, and after every skirmish going in to tea with buzzing, stinging fingers – gardening gloves or no gardening gloves. After about three years of this, weeding settled down into the everyday preoccupation known to all gardeners, and it has seemed a comparative relaxation ever since my nettling experiences.

Stupidly, I have never managed to handle a hoe. Jabbing away inaccurately with the sharp edge I have wounded or even sliced through the stems of so many plants, and missed so many weeds, that I rarely use one now. At ground level though, using a trowel and my fingers, I am prepared to spend hours in hand-to-hand combat. Each type of weed has its own individual grip on the soil and one learns the tiny techniques that make them loosen their grasp. A sharp flick, a steady pull, a gentle twist or a deep scoop – all are part of the relentless tactics of hand weeding. Only to another gardener could one admit to the foolish quickening of the pulse as one follows the tenacious root of a weed, the chagrin when it breaks off and the triumph when it pulls out whole.

A double advantage of having a garden that is really too large is that one can both choose and change one's tasks during a day's gardening. I might start a day with a hankering to do some tying or staking. There are guaranteed to be at least half a dozen plants that are in need of tying-in and will be the better for it forever. (Forever means, until next season.) If it is a wall climber, say a jasmine or a honeysuckle, which is sprawling and needs tackling, the wall wires themselves may need renewing or extending. Next, one must disentangle the stems, separating the strong from the weak, encouraging the new shoots to spread in likely directions and tying them back on to the lines of wire. If the plant must stay really close to the wall, the forward-angled shoots have to be snipped out as well as the weak ones. A well-shaped climber, each stem with its own share of support and light, is a satisfying sight in winter, with its reward yet to come.

Or if I fancy a morning's weeding I need only walk outside with handfork and trowel, and start work. There is never no weeding to do. I try to keep to my resolution of having two barrows, or at least two containers, beside me while I weed. One is for the compost heap, with annual and leafy weeds and dead heads, and the other for perennial weeds and any woody or thorny stems. These go on the bonfire. Separating them saves time and trouble in the long run, but with one's nose buried in a flowerbed it is easier to go on forking, clearing, snipping and throwing the weeds behind one, than to turn round and put them in their proper places.

But the most fun in gardening can be in its variety of tasks. If I am down in the orchard, clearing a space for the little cyclamen that are getting smothered under the *Viburnum fragrans*, I might notice a damaged branch on one of the fruit trees. This needs the pruning saw that is kept in the granary but may have been left in the kitchen. In the course of that round trip I am likely to notice a dozen other jobs, some needing a moment, others an hour, all urgent and all completely different. If a paeony needs a fresh stake, that's another trip to the granary. Crossing the terrace to get to the granary, I see that a recently-moved pansy is wilting and thirsty, and the

watering can is over by the herb garden. Between the
terrace and the herb garden, goodness knows what
priorities will appear. If I am strong minded I will go
straight back to the cyclamen in the orchard and
begin at the beginning. But there is a delight in
spending a day doing what comes next to hand in a
haphazard way. It is also easier physically because you
are constantly using different sets of muscles, instead
of working your back, wrist or knees to the point of
exhaustion. This means that by the end of the day you
are aching all over instead of in one or two places, but
you do recover sooner.

Pruning, though, is something I could do all day long.
Naturally there are appropriate times to prune
different plants but there is quite a lot one can do in
the summer as well as at the beginning and end of
winter. The summer-flowering shrubs are in fact the
easiest to deal with because they are so perfectly
consistent. To change a shrub that has finished
flowering and is drooping and overblown into a clear
outline of next year's promise is a constructive job
undertaken in June. Following a flowered branch
back, you find next year's shoot immediately behind
it, all ready to grow on through the summer. A
pruning cut a quarter of an inch above it gives the
shoot the light and air to let it go ahead strongly.
Once that is done, it is easier to see where the more
ruthless pruning needs to be done – a few of the
older stems that need taking out at ground level, then
the weak and straggly ones, as well as any that are
crossing or tangled.

 By this time I tend to get trigger-happy with the
secateurs, and have to stand back at a distance to take

a good look. A little artistic shaping is all very well, but it is easy to get carried away and find oneself left with a sadly cropped little shrub. Spiraeas, kolkwitzias, philadelphus, weigelas – all are satisfying shrubs to prune. Once the old flowering shoots are gone one can forget that a whole year must pass before they bloom again, and look for a moment at a healthy well-shaped plant before it melts into the background. Some trick of eye and mind renders practically invisible everything in the garden whose season is done, so that one's glance slips across to the flowers whose turn is next. Provided, that is, the old shoots are pruned away, the lupins cut down, the pansies dead-headed. Fortunately the aesthetic side of this task coincides with the plants' well-being, so that their growing energy is not wasted on seeding. I wonder whether those shrubs which we grow for their autumn glamour, their seedheads or hips, would be much larger if we consistently cut them too after flowering. My *rugosa* roses, for instance, look very healthy at about five feet, but if I dead-headed them for a couple of years perhaps they would be eight feet tall. However, I doubt it. They would probably be outraged.

(No, I don't hold conversations with plants. I give them occasional instructions when I plant them, such as, 'There, you've had everything you could possibly want. Now just get on and grow.' Or if they have been damaged, and need to be trimmed back past a broken branch or stem, I do urge them, 'Try to think of it as pruning.' This sometimes works. Apart from that, it is merely a case of, 'Oh *do* try.' Or, 'Oh, well done.' That hardly counts as conversation.)

The old roses, although they are never pruned, do respond to selective shortening of their longest shoots, back to a new bud. I only do this to help define next year's shape or to take off some of the extra length that is liable to crack or suffer in the winter. It surprises me that the stems of shrub roses, whose natural habit is to overlap and tangle, should be so intolerant of rubbing or scraping against each other. They form callouses and weaknesses very easily, and at these points they will break or allow diseases to enter. Perhaps this is a natural form of pruning when they grow in the wild.

The job of dead-heading the shrub roses occupies several days in July for me. As a process it is somewhere between pruning and cutting back, but is not quite either of those things, and is very hard work. A few of the old shrub roses will have a small repeat flowering much later, and in my garden 'Louise Odier' wins the prize for this, with brave pink blooms until October, smaller and frailer than in June, but very welcome.

The climbing roses eventually grow beyond pruning, but in their earlier years I try to establish some order by pruning after they flower. Every year I 'let down' one or two of the climbers out of a tree or off a wall, and spread it out across the ground. Then I prune out its oldest and weakest shoots and put it back up again. This is quite a formidable project and even a delicate rose like 'Félicité et Perpétue' can be half a day's work. And *Rosa filipes* when it is approached turns into a monster and a bully. Its thorns do not even wait for me to stretch out my arm towards them. I am sure they actively attack me and can inflict more vicious wounds than any rose I know. I have finally found that I can offer my *filipes* a reasonable amount of space to take up its high arching shape by leaving only five big shoots coming from the ground. Every few years I put on a long shiny mac, gumboots, a riding hat, and the sort of gloves that a falcon might safely perch on. Then I move in with long-handled pruners and a saw. Huge woody stems are destroyed and dragged off to the bonfire. The next year it flowers with gentle abandon and the winter's thorny battle is quite forgotten.

There is one paradox about pruning that I have not yet come to terms with. Sometimes a shrub or a small tree is weaker or thinner on one side and shows signs of becoming unbalanced as it grows. The obvious remedy is to prune the branches harder on the strong side, to give the weak side a chance to catch up. But the theory of pruning to encourage growth tells me to prune the weak side harder so that it will respond more energetically. I am rarely strongminded enough to do this, nor am I certain which line to take in individual cases. I think I know the answer – it all depends.

Cutting back, as opposed to pruning, can be a problem. One year, determined to be neat and tidy by the end of December, I killed a lot of grey-leaved plants by cutting them back too early. The weather was mild enough to stimulate new soft growth which was then vulnerable when the hard frosts came. Now I leave my grey-leaved plants, many of which are not quite shrubs and not quite hardy, to look untidy till the spring. The exceptions are senecio, which can be clipped into shape at any time without apparently taking offence, and southernwood (*Artemisia abrotanum*) which gets a hard cut almost to the ground every autumn. By March there are minute pinpoints of green all over the old stems, and by May the beautifully fragrant shoots are back again like upright feathers of greeny-grey.

Summer pruning does not coincide with serious feeding, but winter pruning or cutting back is a good time for a heavy feed. I am fortunate to have access to a load of farmyard manure every year. Most of the roses get three or four large spadefuls each winter and so do other shrubs, either when they are young or looking less than flourishing. In the herbaceous beds the paeonies get a feed of muck and so do the hellebores. The vines always have a heavy feed, while the clematis get a smaller dollop. Some of my load is used at the bottom of planting holes, and young hostas seem to appreciate it too. The hellebores get their share as soon as it arrives in October because some of them, the *H. atrorubens* and even some of the varieties of *H. orientalis*, are in flower by Christmas. However neatly we distribute the muck round the roots of a plant, it will look hopelessly untidy within a week. The blackbirds and thrushes move in and pick it over, spreading chunks of manure and straw for yards around.

HELLEBORUS ORIENTALIS
Their dark reds, dusky pinks and pure whites all have distinctive and individual markings inside the flower. Books and catalogues usually describe them only as 'variable'. I would call them exquisite, romantic and without equal.

Muck-spreading is very hard work. Fortunately for me, Malcolm is able to take on most of it because mowing is finished by the end of October. He believes firmly in the use of organic fertiliser and distributes it with great energy and generosity. He knows that I will come fussing along afterwards with a handfork to ensure that young shoots are not bruised and that bulbs will be able to find their way through later. It is not an equal division of labour because he does all the really hard part of it, but at least he gets it done faster if I restrict myself to following along behind, although the blackbirds and I have our separate aims as we follow in Malcolm's footsteps.

Apart from this slightly annoying habit of minor extra muck-spreading, birds do very little damage, even though we are hosts to so many in the course of a year. One year we had a family of sixteen French partridges parading about the garden. They did surprisingly little harm and slept in the marjoram. They are foolish birds, despite their immaculate and sophisticated markings and eye make-up, and proved it the next year when they nested on the edge of the tennis court. My family are used to being asked to avoid various corners when we find active nests, but it is not easy to play tennis on tiptoe. However, the partridges sat on, unperturbed, pretending to be invisible, until one night, inevitably, a dog or a fox got the whole lot. The nest, which wasn't much of a nest anyway, was scattered, and for many weeks the disconsolate parents wandered round the garden with their heads in the air, as though they were trying to remember what it was they were meant to be looking after.

Mice have not been too much trouble since I stopped growing vegetables. Their one predilection is for the Christmas roses, *Helleborus niger*, as opposed to the *H. orientalis*. These grow alongside each other in the little dairy garden against the north side of the house. I cannot tell whether these hellebores actually taste different to a mouse, or whether the buds of *H. niger* are singled out because they are nearer to the ground. The succulent-looking necks of *H. niger* curve closely against the ground for a month or so before the flower heads lift up and open, and very often the buds are nibbled right off at the neck. Meanwhile, the *H. orientalis* are never touched.

The most troublesome invaders are not mice, but moles. Not because of their hills, which I don't mind very much as long as they are not in the centre of a lawn. One has to admire the way they shoulder through the stoniest ground to throw up the finest soil. It would take me hours to extract a bowlful of such soil and I am always impressed by their powerful labours. On the other hand it depresses me to think that the mole probably doesn't even know he has left me a molehill – while I can at least scoop up the soil and use it.

Their really destructive habit is to follow the watering-can in dry weather. When a young plant is in need of watering I can almost feel the moles hurrying along under my feet, burrowing towards the damp patch of ground. When I investigate a shrub that looks unhappy in its first season I often find that, although there is no tell-tale molehill, a mole has been tunnelling in the moist earth round about. The young roots, carefully and recently firmed into the ground, are waving about in a little hollow cave. There seems to be no answer to this because without watering, the

plant would wilt anyway before its roots were well
down. At the first sign of drought I have to keep
checking that watered plants are firm in the ground
and not being undermined.

Rabbits do even more harm. Even if we fenced the
whole circumference of the garden they would still
walk in at the gate. The damage they do is in some
respects controllable. All the young trees have to have
guards on their trunks, or netting if they are not tall
enough for a guard. Very young bark is evidently the
most tasty. After three or four years' growth I find that
the low branches of small willows or shrubs are no
longer nibbled unless there is snow on the ground.
The rabbits come in from the fields in the cold
weather, hoping to find more food and shelter in the
garden, and apart from their nasty trick of debarking,
they also nibble certain plants to the ground. Two
years ago half the pinks in the border were bitten
down over and over again. I didn't cover them in case
that would only encourage the rabbits to move on to
more and more plants. I don't think they had a
particular liking for pinks; rather that they had found
a quiet corner at the back of the border, and could
nibble at the nearest green shoots without venturing
out very far. One year the polyanthus were singled
out for this attention. I discovered a hare's form
under the big old senecio nearby, which gave the
hare perfect cover, and a good larder of polyanthus
for several feet around.

I have since scrapped those polyanthus, not because
of the hare, but because of their (the polyanthus', not
the hare's) promiscuous breeding habits in the
vicinity of primroses. I had originally a good little

clump of primroses, grown from a small root I once
stole sentimentally from the side of Loch Lomond,
and these were growing fairly close to the dozen or
so polyanthus that I put in round the senecio. The
polyanthus were bright and cheerful, and a good
mixture of strong colours. Because they flowered
later I thought they would not conflict with the
primroses which were merely their sweet pale selves.
But within two years there arrived seeded plants that
were between polyanthus and primrose in form and,
much more important, the colours had mixed.
Although there are still some clear ones, the effect is
spoiled by vaguely mauve or dark-yellow flowers
interspersed and seeding with the others so that the
whole palette is muddied. I am sure that part of a
gardener's work is to be ruthless.

The other side of that coin is Moving. Nobody tells
you about Moving in the gardening books, yet it is
one of the most creative and satisfying of the autumn
jobs in my garden. I think it rates a capital letter, the
verb to Move being an activity of such constructive
significance to me. ('Done any good Moving this
autumn?') Moving is an admission that I am not very
good at visualising the effect of an association of
plants in advance. After all these years I am still a
sticker-inner. But when I have to recognise that I was
wrong the first time, at least I can see what might
work better, and have a second chance through some
judicious Moving. And a plant that is not thriving in a
particular setting can have a second chance too.
Sometimes a small plant is in danger of being
swamped by its more vigorous neighbour, or needs
more shade, or perhaps less shade. If only one can

remember to Move in November what was so obvious
in June. It is one of the aspects of gardening that really
does need a pencil and a suitable piece of paper
rather than a crumpled scrap in a jeans pocket.

Even roses and shrubs Move quite easily in their
first few years if they are cut down short in their
resting season. I know it is said that one rose should
never be planted where another has been before, but
I have found that a new rose can take the place of
another quite satisfactorily if the new one is given an
extra large hole with some fresh earth in it and plenty
of fertiliser and bone meal.

The two single summer jobs without which the
garden would not survive at all, are the mowing and
the spraying. Both are expertly undertaken by one or
other of the Malcolms in turn. The first cut of the year,
when the grass begins to grow in April, is as
encouraging an occasion as the day the clocks go
forward and from then on the garden is waking up.
None of my grass is of very good quality. There is too
much of it in proximity to the fields to tackle all the
weeds and moss successfully, but it takes a very dry
summer to spoil its greenness. To see the lawns cut in
early spring is like seeing a pony emerge with glossy
flanks and clean lines from its shaggy winter coat.

Sometimes I catch myself feeling complacent about
how my roses keep free of greenfly and mildew and
wonder why people make such a fuss about these
pests and blights. Then I remember that at absolutely
regular intervals, from spring onwards, Malcolm is
quietly padding about with his spray. A few
herbaceous plants are vulnerable too, and they get a
useful going-over at the appropriate moment. Aphids

of various colours tend to attack the herbaceous
flowers rather late in the summer. The blackfly go for
the big white daisies; most Michaelmas daisies and
the woolly grey lamb's tongue, *Stachys lanata*, are
very prone to mildew. An exception among the
Michaelmas daisies is *Aster × frikartii* which is
mildew-resistant. It has a more shrubby habit than
most Michaelmas daisies, and bright blue single
flowers with golden stamens. Very cheerful and
useful, it has a long flowering season throughout the
late summer.

Much as I hate to reach the end of the mowing season,
when the grass stops growing quite suddenly and the
cattle have to be taken off the fields, there are
compensations in the garden work. The Malcolms can
turn their attention to the jobs we have plotted during
the summer. Paths can be reshaped, gates mended,
walls and posts dealt with – all the changes to the
framework that will make the difference to the next
year.

Maintaining a garden is a constant trade-off with
nature and the elements. The right fertiliser at the
wrong time might be disastrous, while a plant left
alone when it should have been cut back sometimes
behaves more beautifully than any of its carefully
pruned neighbours. I used to have an ageing ash tree,
and four years ago it died. I had previously planted a
miniature climbing China rose called 'Pompom de
Paris' against it, and a 'Perle d'Azur' clematis was also
climbing, but with only moderate enthusiasm, into its
lower branches. Instead of taking the tree out I cut it
to a stump five feet high, leaving it as a support until I
should have decided whether (and where) to try to

move the rose and the clematis. For some months I left them alone. In June they astonished me by deciding to flower simultaneously and in great profusion, and they continued to do so for at least six weeks. Their flowers were completely intermingled to the height of the tree stump and then sprayed out separately. The tiny double pink-quartered blooms of 'Pompom de Paris' lay in dense clusters against their stems, and 'Perle d'Azur's' flowers were widely-spreading violet stars. The tones of the pink and blue were exactly complementary, while the shapes of the two blooms were exactly contrasting. Although the rose should be short and the clematis should grow very tall, the proportions were perfect and the effect was a stunning serendipity of 'Pompom' and 'Perle'. Since then I have taken the greatest care of these two plants and kept the old tree stump in place for them. Yet they have never again flowered with a quarter of that abundance and have scarcely overlapped in their flowering. 'Pompom de Paris' is always nearly over before the clematis comes into flower, and the clematis itself looks a bit scruffy nowadays, needing more height.

However, in general, of course, it does not do to ignore the needs of plants, especially when the cold weather begins and the main tasks are to protect. The early frosts are a shock every year. The garden seems unprepared because so many soft green leaves suddenly blacken and fall. Dry cold weather and snow seem to be the less unfriendly attributes of winter and the short days can be still and harmless. At ground level small plants and crowns are safely tucked away when snow falls, but thick snow may still damage the boughs of shrubs and small trees. It may even break them if they are evergreen and supporting a heavy weight of it. At least it is fun to knock snow from branches with a broom or a rake to let them spring up again.

Wind and ice are far more malevolent. When snow melts into wet ground and then refreezes, ice crystallises deep into roots and underground stems which may never recover. Cold winds at the same time rock plants with too much exposed growth, and with their roots loosened by frost they are tugged and strained and hurt. Just as in the spring, staking tends to fall into the category of good intentions, only dealt with when a good deal of flopping about makes the need obvious. As I struggle with canes and string I resolve that next year every plant will stand to attention, and remind myself how much easier it is to stake when plants are still young. Likewise before the winter winds blow hard. It pays to be strong-minded about shortening long sprays of roses and shrubs quite apart from any other reasons for pruning. Even this job needs qualifying, though. The branches of some plants are better left to bend and whip flexibly so long as the roots are held securely.

I have become a little more philosophical about hard weather, but during the first two or three planting seasons I used to watch in outrage and despair as winter descended on the garden. I was baffled by frost damage because I found that even a sheltered south-west corner could be more vulnerable to frost than exposed and windy places. Then Pat explained to me that I should think of frost like water, running downhill and collecting in low-lying pockets. If there were a hole at the bottom of my south-west wall the frost would actually run away through it. I will take her word for this – I have

enough trouble with holes in walls without making
any more. So the particular south-west corner I have
in mind with its tender young (and very expensive)
Carpenteria californica has a winter bulkhead of
straw and netting rigged up in Heath Robinson
fashion.

I was given a tip by Malcolm about protecting
plants with straw. At first I used hay, which seemed
cosier for them and is nicer to handle. It did not occur
to me until Malcolm pointed it out that hay is full of
seeds, so I was sowing a fine crop of weeds for the
next spring. Now I use straw which is only dry stalks,
and try to peg it down with netting against the wind
and the birds.

Another useful lesson I learned from Malcolm was
the danger of planting very early-flowering shrubs
against an east-facing wall. After a very cold night the

flowers of, say, japonica, may be scorched by warming up too quickly if they face the rising sun. Gardening is so logical.

In late June, during the shrub-rose season, there comes a day when the garden is Open. The first year this happened I had agreed with some misgiving to join the scheme but was very flattered to have been asked. When the day finally arrived I lost courage and went upstairs to the attic to shut myself in. At five past two (we opened at two o'clock) I peeped out of the attic window and was appalled to see a family of total strangers walk across the lawn and sit down on one of my garden seats. After a while the mother brought out her knitting and the father began to walk about peering at the flowers, while the children pottered around looking bored. Along the drive I could see more people approaching, another family and two women, and I wondered whether I should have a nervous breakdown.

By two thirty I summoned up sufficient nerve to take another look out of the window. Quite a crowd of people were wandering about. They looked rather calm and reasonable, strolling around and chatting. One couple were kissing behind the viburnum but only I, from my vantage point, could see them. I plucked up courage and tried mingling. Before long I was exchanging garden talk and having a very good time.

It is difficult to imagine what other people see when they look at one's own garden, whose contours are so completely familiar, and I find it very instructive. Any visitor approaching someone else's flowerbed with interest will see its whole proportion and notice the conspicuous features and the relationships within it. Approaching one's own flowerbed one's eye is already skimming over most of the plants and looking out for a peculiarity – a favourite or a weakling, a new addition or a problem. Watching people walk around on Open Day, even indulging in a little surreptitious eavesdropping, I found I could teach myself a fresh view and learn from the constructive comments of other gardeners.

I also realised that everyone who comes, except for a few dragged-along children, does so because they like looking at gardens, which is a good start. Even when hundreds of people turn up, which they may do on a fine day, they don't all come at once. When six o'clock comes and they have all gone home, I walk round; never once have I found any litter or a single damaged plant. It does become less of an ordeal to open the garden as the years go by, although I feel apprehensive for weeks beforehand. The whole place looks shabby and weedy to me, and the wrong things are in flower, and I dread the thought of so many people coming in. Then, being contrary, when the day arrives, I desperately want the sun to shine and lots of people to pay their fifty pence at the gate.

But the value of Open Day, so far as the garden itself is concerned, is the annual spit-and-polish that has to be done and that is so good for it. The thought of visitors making critical comparisons opens my eyes to neglected corners and untidy beds. Even the compost heap gets straightened a bit. I have learned too that the one job that makes more difference than any other is to clip the edges of the lawns where they meet the flowerbeds. This gives a miraculously spruced-up impression, however temporarily. I have long accepted that the day will never dawn when I can look around me and find nothing urgent waiting to be done. The garden imposes its own priorities, and my plans are constantly overtaken. In practice, I work in whichever place is about to reach its best moment, and the rest must take its turn apart from the cosmic efforts that lead up to Open Day.

It can be disconcerting to hear visitors so frequently tell me, 'It's very informal, isn't it?' in surprised tones. Formality is by no means my style, but the repeated comment makes me wonder whether garden-goers are not only careful people and good about litter, but also, being very polite and kindly, choose to use words like 'informal', rather than 'slightly untidy', or 'a complete mess'.

For me, the practice of gardening is indeed still a matter of practising; and trial and error, always a factor in gardening, still exercise a very large influence on my year's efforts. Many of my errors can be hidden to a certain extent in extravagant replacements. It is far too late now, fortunately, for me to keep account of how much I spent on the garden in the first years. Had I done so I am quite sure that I would be a more skilled propagator by now, far more patient, and thus less wasteful.

The theory of gardening is a very different matter, and I learned gradually how to use the books and the catalogues. A simple key is to come to terms with the fact that the catalogues always bring the good news, while the books, being more objective, may bring you the bad news too. The job of a catalogue is to sell plants, and although I am easily tempted by a catalogue description I have found that it is salutary to take a second, more cautious, view from the gardening books. If, for instance, I am looking for a

specially good white form of a herbaceous plant, I
might spot one in a catalogue that promises 'a delicate
ivory' or 'palest cream' flower. Before being quite
swept away, a quick glance at Ward Lock's *Complete
Gardening* could reveal that a dismissive and
uncompromising 'off-white' describes the identical
variety. Then I have to think for myself about what I
really am looking for, and what I am likely to get. After
all, off-white may be just what I need.

When I started planting I was given the name of
Scott's nurseries at Merriott in Somerset, and at once
found I had been well advised. I was ordering
herbaceous plants by the dozen and half dozen then,
plus shrubs, trees and old-fashioned roses. Scott's
catalogue, halfway in size to a book, became my most
immediate reference source. Their descriptions,
particularly of flowering shrubs, are helpful and
down to earth. If you choose one kind of
philadelphus against another, or want to select a
shrub of a particular proportion or colour, their
catalogue gives accurate descriptions with some
useful comments thrown in for good measure.

Robert Allwood of Scott's, whose father was the
famous breeder of pinks, is constantly working to
keep a wide range of plants available. The garden
centres can produce limited ranges more cheaply,
and of course greater variety means greater wastage,
so the competition for the traditional nurseries is
fierce. Sending out thousands of plants every season
makes packaging and transport problematical. We
think of container-grown plants as a comparatively
recent technique, but Mr Allwood told me that his
father always sent out plants in containers, and that
delivery of bare-root plants was only later thought of,
being a way of sending orders with less weight and
therefore less expense by rail. He now sends his

plants with soil again, and feels that they are less at
risk on replanting. Lifting stock without earth means
that the little hair roots are lost. Going back into the
ground later in the season may leave too little time for
plants to make good hair roots again before they have
to start growing shoots. 'This,' warns Mr Allwood,
means there is 'too much demand on top.' He also
reminded me that plants grown in peaty containers
need extra watering, even soaking before planting,
because they are liable to be dried out during
transport, and water tends to float off the top of the
peat and run away round the sides.

A wide-ranging catalogue which is consistent in
every detail is hard to guarantee; stocks will
occasionally fail or be sold out, and nothing can
hasten their replacement. But Mr Allwood has
emphatic advice for anyone starting to plant a garden
or part of a garden. 'Plan a framework of good
common stock,' he says, 'and then fill in with the
better stuff.'

There are still great nurseries like Scott's all over
the country – Notcutts, Bressingham, Sherards and
many more, which will surely survive despite the
garden centre boom. Beth Chatto with her individual
vision has a mouth-watering catalogue which she
backs up with an irresistible stand at the Chelsea
Show. Chelsea, for all its bulging claustrophobic
pressure, can be revealing, and I have been
introduced to small specialist nurseries there that I
would otherwise never have heard of. Each has its list
of treasures; some may specialise in particular plants
only, others may be specialist as opposed to ordinary.
These are the real favourites for me, each full of
interesting and original varieties and bearing the
imprint of the plantsmen who have built up their
collections. If one of these nurseries is within range,

an hour's visit, even only once or twice a year, can be worth any amount of browsing in catalogues. There are one or two near me, and every visit is a treat. They are the places to hunt for a particular viola, seen and admired in a friend's garden, or to pick up by chance a small fern that would fill a tricky corner. 'Treasures' do not mean rarities to me, but especially choice varieties of plants that I particularly like.

Here are a handful of those favourites, mainly, but not all, from the Chelsea Show:

Garsdon Mill of Malmesbury in Wiltshire has a small but very attractive list of ornamental trees and shrubs.

Robert Bowlby of Reigate in Surrey sells bulbs which are mainly small with a great collection of fritillaries. I usually go there for presents or special treats.

Avon Bulbs of Bathford also goes in for unusual and beautiful bulbs, both large and small.

Christopher Lloyd of Great Dixter near Northiam in Sussex has a list of his clematis collection and also of herbaceous plants and shrubs which are sure to be high class.

Robinson's Gardens of Sevenoaks in Kent offer a bit of everything in their catalogue, all well described.

Careby Manor in Lincolnshire has mainly small plants and alpines, listing many unusual herbaceous plants.

Ingwersons of Gravetye in East Sussex includes a big choice of hebes, saxifrages and dianthus with a large selection of other herbaceous plants.

Parker Jervis at Longworth in Oxfordshire is fortunately within half an hour's drive for me. Their catalogue combines specialist plants with a very broad collection. They define their specialism as 'anything that is not ordinary' and the result seems to be a whole range of treasures, mostly small in stature and often changing so that every visit reveals new delights.

Washfield Nursery at Hawkhurst in Kent is run by Elizabeth Strangman. I have already mentioned that my sister Pat has brought me original and beautiful plants from this interesting small nursery. Birthday presents from Pat tend to be container-grown and usually come from Washfield. They are inevitably special and unusually beautiful. Perhaps a recent form of campanula, a frilly miniature alchemilla, a lovely *Cosmos atropurpurea* (the hot-chocolate plant) or one more hellebore with even more beautiful markings than the last, because she is constantly breeding new forms of these. With Elizabeth Strangman growing them, and Pat choosing them, my birthday presents are all 'stars' to be found here and there around the garden.

On my way home from London, near Oxford, is Waterperry Horticultural Centre, which has a great appeal for me. It was started in the thirties by Miss Havergal as a training school for horticulturalists and gardeners, and this is still its first function. The gardens are an example of how an enterprise can be improved by commercial need. The nursery, very far from a modern garden centre, has increased greatly, selling plants that have been grown on the premises

and are brought out for sale at the right moment. Staff
and students are working to a high standard and you
feel that every plant you buy will be a healthy,
well-grown specimen. Some are in containers and
those that are bare-rooted are not bare at all, but well
dug into soil beds, from which you can fork them out
yourself.

Waterperry is not particularly specialist except for
its vast collection of Kabschia 'cushion' saxifrages
which was started by Valerie Finnis. The real pleasure
of Waterperry is in walking round the gardens
themselves, where you see in their seasons
beautifully grown versions of the plants you can buy
at planting time. Herbaceous plants, shrubs, alpines
and conifers are all there. There is a border of
Michaelmas daisies of every colour and height, which
is magnificent in September against a high brick wall.
Stock beds lie alongside those that are used for
garden planting. Grass paths lead between the rows
of skilfully trained apples and pears in espaliers and
fans, with soft fruit beyond them. The atmosphere of
the place is relaxed and friendly, but one is
nevertheless conscious that the people there are
trying to grow plants in perfect condition. I find it an
exceptional place. A visit to Waterperry gives me a
chance to see plants growing where they can speak
for themselves and where neither book nor catalogue
is needed. I know there are many nurseries large and
small where one can walk in adjoining gardens but
most of these I only know by reputation or rare visits.

In armchair gardening I often find that instead of
browsing through the catalogues, I discover a
much-desired plant in a gardening book, which leads

me to the reverse process – that of searching through the catalogues. This search is sometimes long, sometimes unfulfilled but usually very informative.

Which books then? Mine fall into categories. The how-to books of detailed instructions and techniques about things like pruning; the specialist books on one species such as irises or snowdrops, or in fact almost any plant you can think of for people with particular interests; the overall compendium books about every aspect of gardening. These last have their different styles and emphasis, and I find Ward Lock's *Complete Gardening* the most comprehensively useful. Its information on cultivation is clear and its descriptions are reliable. The *Reader's Digest Encyclopaedia of Garden Plants and Flowers* is alphabetically organised, and I find that invaluable too. I much prefer it to their *Gardening Year* which tells me what I should be doing each month. If I happen to look at the instructions for March in April I realise how much trouble I am already in. Either I know it by now or I would rather not be told.

Best of all are the books which are written for the sake of their subject but read for the sake of reading. They manage to encompass text book information and poetry in the space of a page and have profound and opposite effects on aspiring gardeners. On optimistic days I am inspired and encouraged by reading them. On pessimistic days they have the effect of opening my eyes to the inadequately cultivated rubbish that straggles along in my so-called garden. Then I have to return to the plants themselves and remember that a rose is, thank goodness, always a rose, and a pansy a pansy, and even my little beech will one day be a real beech tree. After a walk round and a spell of weeding my nerve returns and I can read on. There is a wealth of these books. Their authors are today's gurus who write for today's gardeners, and they are realistic about both the scope and the limitations of gardening today. They are devoted to the subject without being pompous, and have great professional knowledge without being pretentious. They make irresistible reading.

From the small but growing collection on my own shelf I would choose this list:

> Lloyd, Christopher: *The Well Tempered Garden* (Viking, 1985). *Adventurous Gardener* (Penguin, 1985). *Clematis* (Collins, 1977).
> Fox, Robin Lane: *Variations on a Garden* (Penguin, 1986). *Better Gardening* (Penguin, 1985).
> Thomas, Graham Stuart: *The Art of Planting* (Dent, 1984). *Old Shrub Roses* (Dent, 1979). *Plants for Ground-cover* (Dent, 1977). *Perennial Garden Plants* (Dent, 1982).

There is just one other book that I would not be without. This is *Origins of Garden Plants* (Constable, 1982), by John Fisher. He writes of the discoverers and explorers who brought plants and seeds from China and Turkey, Tibet and New Zealand and every inaccessible corner of the world. The history of their amazing and brave adventures is described alongside the patient scientific cataloguing that produced the great plant classifications that we now know. It is an inspiring book, and after reading it every gardener must look with new respect at the flowers, so homely and so familiar, blooming so unremarkably in his garden.

11

Time and the Place

hen we bought the house at Minster Lovell I did not feel that we owned the garden too, only that we had the right to a stake in it. I had hoped to find ground that had been as little cultivated as possible, not wanting to inherit someone else's garden ready-made. Having no earlier experience, I had no preconceived plans either. The idea of having scope and limitations was new to me, and themes came only gradually into focus. Even the seasons took me by surprise. As months passed I found myself bombarded by successive emotional experiences – the sensuousness of summer, the nostalgia and melancholy of autumn and winter, and finally spring again, when Larkin's trees begin 'Afresh, afresh, afresh!'

Every gardener responds to the demands of the seasons, and Vita Sackville-West was one of the great interpreters of the year's changing moods. Her artist's eye was specially focused on gardens, from individual plants to the design and essence of a garden. She wanted to explain her personal vision to the world at large. Because of her, people looked more closely, not necessarily liking the same things, but discovering the reasons for their own tastes. She looked for the natural best that any plant had to offer, and encouraged that. If she recognised in pansies that their virtue lay in a sweet disorder, she somehow ensured that at Sissinghurst pansies would be the sweetest and the most disordered. And if a certain tree could offer a stately or a graceful shape, she could see how to place it so that it would grow to its best advantage.

My sister's small village garden, as opposite as could be in scale and style from Sissinghurst, has just this quality. Every plant in it is happy. Each is the best variety of its kind, growing to its healthiest potential, and with the best possible neighbours. That degree of finesse is a gift. Gardening is like a game, to be played with great skill, and to a certain extent it can be taught. There are some who play the game instinctively, and many for whom the rules are always elusive. Even more, and among them I include myself, struggle along between triumphs and disasters. We try to be mindful of long-term effects while submerged in the work in hand. A failure is usually easy to define and understand. The lesson can be learned – an association changed or a placing improved. But how much more thought-provoking it is to succeed. The satisfaction of an intention achieved is straightforward enough. But it is the moments of magic that are not to be explained. They may be captured by the vision and skill of a Sackville-West; for me, however, they are rare, and I know perfectly well that they are as likely to be fortuitous as planned.

Of course the magic is not entirely in the moment. It may be lasting and unchanging, but it has often struck me that light, particularly that of long evenings, can be the transforming influence that imbues a scene, however fleetingly, with magic. Garden magic, or at least mystery, goes hand-in-hand with romance, and then we feel the pleasure of it all. Sometimes Peter and I walk down to the pools and if he is feeling particularly pleased with them he will say, 'How wonderful to see the Ruins and the church and the sky all reflected in the water.' This makes me laugh because unlike him I keep my soul in my gumboots, and I ask him why he has spent hundreds of pounds so that he can see all that upside down, when we can always see it the right way up for nothing. But when the fountain is playing and the waterfall splashing I

think I see what he means, especially when I think of
Auden's line, 'So restful yet so festive'.

I have always thought of my garden as a new addition
to an old place, but in fact that cannot be my claim.
Perhaps the medieval garden at Minster Lovell was
less organised and less pampered than mine, but I
have no real evidence even of that. In the Middle
Ages, of course, they did not have the benefits that we
enjoy of vastly developed hybridisation. Variations
would have appeared with naturally-occurring
hybrids, but many of those must have died out. The
great scope of gardening today, so much of which lies
in the quality and quantity of hybrid garden plants
and in their availability, is thanks to the skills and
techniques of modern nurserymen.

But some of the local ladies of medieval times may
have been just as committed to their plants as I am.
They would have exchanged cuttings, collected seeds
and tried out new forms of violas. Sharp scythes could
have trimmed finer lawns than mine, long before
mowing machines were invented. Honeysuckles and
dog roses would have grown in abundance and there
would certainly have been fruit trees. Primroses and
cowslips probably in far greater profusion than mine.
Lavender and foxgloves would have been familiar
sights as well as many more of the plants that I cultivate
today. My collection of herbs, in fact, must be meagre
compared with those in a medieval herb garden.

This was brought forcibly home to me in 1985, when
English Heritage, by imaginatively designating a week

in July as Tudor 500, caused the fifteenth century to come to life in my garden in a most unusual way. The date was chosen to commemorate the battle of Bosworth Field half a millennium before, and Tudor 500 re-enacted the life of Minster Lovell Hall in 1485.

The year was a very bad one in these parts. There was disaster and hardship because Francis Lovell, who was then the Lord in the big house, had fought on the losing side in that battle, suffering defeat with Richard III.

With immense and detailed care, the occasion was re-created in the Ruins by craftsmen, teachers, historians and curators. It was my good fortune that they had two worries: where to store equipment during their preparations, and what to do in case of rain. The simple answer was to open the gate between the Ruins and the garden so that the tithe barn could play its part, offering storage space and, if necessary, shelter.

Fortunately the whole week was fine. Every morning successive coachloads of schoolchildren arrived from far and wide, to be turned into instant peasants. In the tithe barn the boys were given brown tunics to wear, and the girls brown dresses with white aprons and caps; all the adults were similarly dressed. The children spent their day sculpting with the stone mason, hammering metal with the smith, and watching the falconer with his birds. A potter built an oven so that they could make pots and fire them; a fletcher showed them how arrows were made. Throughout each day they watched and took part, all the while absorbing the story of 1485. Lunch was eaten on the grass in the Ruins. Here, they served each other with food they had cooked on charcoal braziers, sweetened with honey and flavoured with herbs, using bowls and platters specially made to medieval designs.

The children loved their outing but they were not the only ones to be given a new glimpse of their heritage by this superb way of teaching history. I watched small groups being taken to learn about the herbs in my herb garden and as they trooped back and forth across the lawn, I looked at their surroundings – and mine – with a feeling that approached precognition.

I understood then why the fifteenth century has always been the period that has dominated the atmosphere of the place for me. Of course the Minster existed before the Middle Ages, and was inhabited for long after. The farmhouse itself has evidently been constantly inhabited. Although people who lived here in other centuries may have made great changes, their influence has made little impression on me. I can visualise life here in the nineteenth century, but there was probably little interest taken in the garden by the tenant farmers who lived in the house then. By the beginning of the nineteenth century Minster Lovell Hall had already been ruined for a hundred years, and must have become sadly overgrown and neglected. The sight, however romantic, would shock our preservationist sensibilities today.

In different parts of the grounds, at different times, a garden must have flourished here; no doubt it went through phases of neglect followed by loving restoration. I think the place has a right to expect that anyone who ventures to put roots down into it should add a flower or two. It has always been a place where people have wanted to live. A sheltered valley, a bend in the river (the 'Favoured Windrush'), and the forest of Wychwood in the background, evidently struck even the Romans (and probably their predecessors) as a desirable site. Some years ago I turned up a Marcus Aurelius coin in the root of an old viburnum, and the Minster Lovell jewel, small brother to the tenth-century Alfred Jewel in gold and bright enamels, is said to have been found in the river nearby.

Occasionally a flicker of activity springs up, breathing life into the old Ruins and linking the centuries. I felt it during our Tudor week as I watched the children gathered in the herb garden, and again in 1977, when the village held a Jubilee barn-dance in the tithe barn. Watching people dancing in the firelight, hearing the fiddlers and the laughter, smelling the smoke and the roast meat – the scene could have been any Harvest Home over the centuries. Although we ourselves were the most transient part of the picture, I think we all felt a comradely sense of continuity, of being included in the historical perspective.

We have, too, a shared awareness of the Ruins. The last person to live there was Thomas Coke. When in 1720 he became very rich and grand, he abandoned Minster Lovell and went off to Norfolk to build Holkham Hall. The deserted Minster became a tempting quarry to the villagers and some of its stone was probably used in the building of every house in the village. There is only one street in Minster Lovell, which is lined with peaceful, well-matured gardens. I have only to walk along it to see that we all respond to the spirit of the place. Individual and different as we are, none of us goes against the grain.

Mine is still a young garden and changing all the time. It demands constant love and attention but still insists on having its own way. It may accept or reject my efforts and it certainly makes its own rules.

What a mysterious occupation it is, making a garden! Aching muscles and torn nails, failures and disappointments are the order of the day. So often I find myself wiping cold rain off my glasses with the corner of a muddy handkerchief. Then no sooner does the rain abate than I am told there is to be a drought. Achievements are transitory. Satisfaction is not even a word in the vocabulary, because a gardener sees with next year's eyes and is never satisfied with this year's blooms.

It is a lifelong battle, with campaigns to be mounted afresh each year against drought and ice, winds and pests, weeds and stones. Yet these are the proper background to garden life, and it is a battle without enemies and without end. Amazingly, you find yourself committed to a primrose and worrying about a pansy. Continuity is all, yet change is all, and once begun you are drawn in for life.

How is it so compelling? Why is it my favourite of all pursuits?

With the dew still on the grass on an early morning in June, a gardener may turn lyrical, and see a garden as a work of art. Work it certainly is. But what art is comparable? What work of art grows and dies, changes its appearance and asserts its own will, fades away and then returns – in fact, lives? Only a garden.

Small wonder, then, that gardening is the purest of pleasures.

Index of Plants

Illustrations and main treatments are indicated by
   page-numbers in **bold** type

Acanthus spinosus **102**
Acer (maple) *palmatum* 66–7; *A. saccharinum* 70–1
Aesculus pavia (Red Buckeye chestnut) 68
Alchemilla mollis **28**, **101**, 108
almond, Russian 65
alpines 26–7, 54–5, weeding 57–8
Anemona pulsatilla **148**, 149
apple-trees 12, **21–4**, 28, **43–6**, 49–52; crab-apple
   50–2
Aralia elata **103**
Arbutus unedo 64
Artemisia abrotanum (Southernwood) 65, 80, 81, 161
arum, bog 110
Aster × *frikartii* 168
astrantia 37

Betula (birch) 31, 66, 144; *B. jacquemontii* **118**
bluebell 87, **143**
bulbs **142–8**
butomus (flowering rush) 110

campanula 29; *C.* 'E.J. Toogood' 26–7
carlina thistle 149
Carpentaria californica **171**
catmint 27, 60, 148
ceanothus 47–9, 80
Chamaecyparis lateralis 55
cistus **55**, 65, 142
Clematis flammula 29; *C. orientalis* 'Bill McKenzie'
   140–1; *C. spooneri* **25**; *C.* 'Marie Boisselot' **129–30**;
   C. 'Perle d'Azur' 168–9; *C.* 'Royal Velours' 35;
   feeding 162
comfrey, Russian 59
cornus (dogwood) 59; *C. alba* 127
Cosmos atrosanguineas 142; *C. atropurpurea* 178
cowslip 89, 185
cyclamen 146, 157, 158
cypress 69
Cytisus battandieri **36**, 37

daisy 38, 150, **168**

delphinium 38, 150
Deutzia elegantissima 64
dicentra 151
dierama ('Angel's Fishing Rod', 'Wand Flower');
   D. pendulum 117; *D. pulcherrimum* **116**, 117
digitalis (foxglove) 63, 64, 89, **149–50**, 185

Echinops ritro 28
Elodea crispa 108, 110, 111, 112–14
epimedium 37
Erythronium dens-canis (dog-toothed violet) **39–40**
Euphorbia epithymoides **27**

fennel **28**, 78, 81, 102
ferns 37, 117
filipendula 110
forget-me-not 17–18, 21, 116
Fritillaria meleagris (Snake's Head Lily) **86**, 87, **144**

Garrya elliptica **104–5**
geranium (cranesbill) 29, 60, 148; *G. endressii* 59,
   135–6; *G. macrorrhizum* 59; *G. phaeum* 37, 136;
   G. pratense **135–6**; *G. sanguineum* 136
grasses 86–7; water 110
gypsophila 28

Hebe hulkeana 65
helianthemum (rock rose) 55
Helleborus atrorubens 37, 162; *H. corsicus* 59, **93–4**;
   H. foetidus 37; *H. niger* 37, 164; *H. orientalis* **35–6**,
   37, **141–2**, **162**, 164; feeding 162
herbs 59, **77–83**
holly 29, 31, 66
hosta 37, 59, 110, 116, **136–7**, 162
Humulus lupulus (hop) 102
Hydrangea petiolaris 37

ipheion 143
iris 29; waterside 109–10; *I. danfordiae* 144;
   I. histriodes 143; *I. kaempferi* 110, 116;
   I. pseudacorus (flag iris) **115**, 116; *I. reticulata* 143,
   144; *I. sibirica* 110

juniper 69

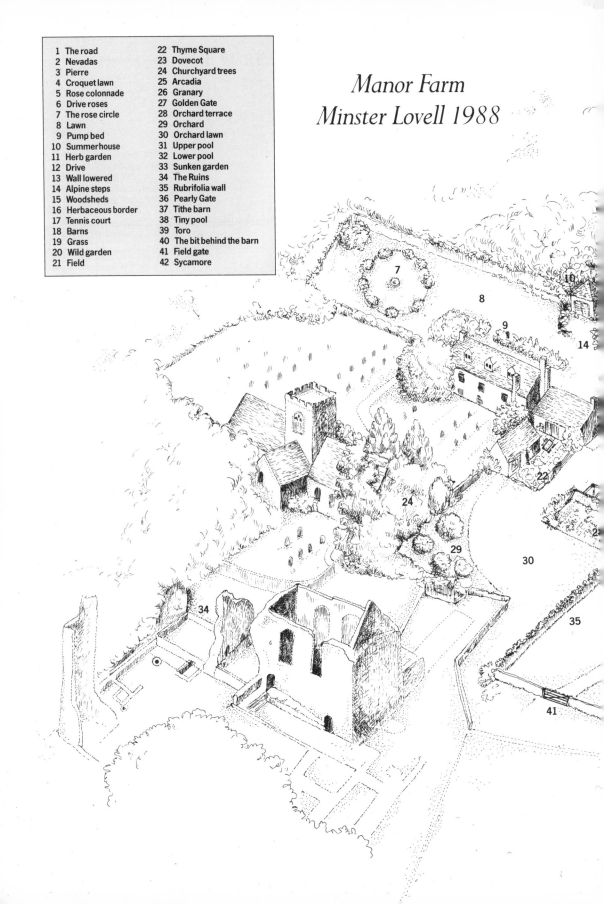

Manor Farm
Minster Lovell 1988

1 The road
2 Nevadas
3 Pierre
4 Croquet lawn
5 Rose colonnade
6 Drive roses
7 The rose circle
8 Lawn
9 Pump bed
10 Summerhouse
11 Herb garden
12 Drive
13 Wall lowered
14 Alpine steps
15 Woodsheds
16 Herbaceous border
17 Tennis court
18 Barns
19 Grass
20 Wild garden
21 Field
22 Thyme Square
23 Dovecot
24 Churchyard trees
25 Arcadia
26 Granary
27 Golden Gate
28 Orchard terrace
29 Orchard
30 Orchard lawn
31 Upper pool
32 Lower pool
33 Sunken garden
34 The Ruins
35 Rubrifolia wall
36 Pearly Gate
37 Tithe barn
38 Tiny pool
39 Toro
40 The bit behind the barn
41 Field gate
42 Sycamore